Preface

"But it's still so young," the puppy's new owners think as they deal with their sweet little dog—and they let the adorable creature get away with murder. That attitude is entirely wrong, however. In the first few months of a puppy's life, it goes through several different stages of development. The experiences it has—or fails to have—in these various phases mold the puppy in very decisive ways.

In this Barron's pet guide, dog owners will learn all they need to know about their puppy's first six months of life to help it become a faithful companion and fit into the family without any difficulties.

In the first part, Katharina Schlegl-Kofler tells how to select a puppy, take care of it, feed it, and keep it healthy. The puppy test she provides will help you find the right pet, the one whose disposition suits you best.

In the second part, the author describes puppies' developmental phases in detail and tells you what to keep an eye on during each phase, so that your pet will become all it can be.

In part three, important rules of training are listed and discussed. Also included is a training program, with the individual exercises explained step by step. Full-color photos and informative drawings bring the text to life.

The author of this book and the editors of Barron's series of pet books wish you a great deal of pleasure as you raise your puppy successfully.

*Please read the
Important Note
on page 63.*

Choosing a Puppy, Helping It Feel at Home, and Caring for It Properly

A 10-week-old puppy. By this age the puppy should already be in its new home.

From Wolf to Dog

Over 10,000 years ago humans brought their first future pet—the wolf—home from the wild. For some time to come, it remained a wild animal that had been tamed. Only over the course of time, through the process of domestication, did it become conditioned to live in a human environment. Thus the wolf became the dog. In this process, two elements combined to make the dog capable of a closer bond to humans than any other domesticated animal: dependence on humans, which was a concomitant of domestication, and a set of social behaviors that still are inherent—as a legacy from the wolf—in dogs today.

Just like the wolf, the dog is dependent upon life in a social unit. For this reason, it also is willing to become a member of such a unit and to observe the rules that are important for life within the group. Major preconditions for the animal's healthy development include close contact with the members of its human pack, as well as living conditions and activities that are appropriate to its species and breed. If these factors are present, the dog will also be willing to accept a two-legged "pack leader."

Many highly critical developmental steps are taken while the dog is still very young. If integration into its human pack and our civilized world is to be successful, proper treatment and support during puppyhood are essential. Your contribution during this crucial time is described in the following chapters.

What You Need to Consider

Dogs—now available in almost 400 different breeds—are among the most popular pets today. Before you decide to make a dog your housemate, however, you need to do a lot of serious thinking. A dog is not an animal that can simply be placed in a cage if need be, like a bird or a rabbit, for example. Nor can you leave a dog home alone all day, like a cat. Quite the contrary: it needs a great deal of attention.

What to consider ahead of time:
• Are you willing to accept responsibility for your pet over a period of 10 years and more, and are you aware that pet ownership entails responsibilities toward your fellow man as well? A dog can't simply be sold again if you lose interest after a few years. Few animals could handle that.
• Are you willing to devote a great part of your free time to your dog and to take it for walks, whether it is raining or storming outside? In addition, there is the time you must spend to train your pet and keep it occupied; such activities are essential parts of

Katharina Schlegl-Kofler

Your Puppy

Expert advice on selecting
a puppy, helping it adapt,
caring for it, and feeding it

With color photographs
by Christine Steimer
and drawings by
György Jankovics

BARRON'S

Contents

Pulling on the same piece of rope is a favorite game of puppies.

Don't be angry. Offering a paw is a gesture of appeasement and submission.

owning a dog and living in harmony with a four-legged partner.

Tip: A full-grown dog can easily spend a few hours alone every day, provided it has been gradually accustomed to doing so, and provided it receives the necessary attention and affection the rest of the time. Puppies and young dogs should only be left alone for short periods until they are about four or five months old. If your job keeps you away from home all day, perhaps you should not have a dog.

• Owning a dog is not inexpensive. Besides the purchase price, which varies greatly depending on the breed, there are the costs of food, accessories such as the collar and leash, a bed or basket to sleep in, and toys. Moreover, you may have to pay an apartment damage deposit and possibly purchase added liability insurance. And don't forget the veterinarian's bills. The dog

Dogs need the kind of care that is appropriate for their species and breed. When choosing a breed, think about what you expect of a dog and what you can offer it.

must be vaccinated once a year and wormed several times a year. If your four-legged companion becomes injured, seriously ill, or needs an operation, the expenses will rapidly mount to hundreds of dollars.

• What will you do with your pet during vacation? If you are unable or unwilling to take the dog along, you need an experienced person or place to look after it during your absence.

• What kind of area do you live in? At a relatively accessible distance, there should be suitable open ground where the dog can run and have a chance to play with other dogs and explore the surroundings.

• Your location and living circumstances also must be taken into account in choosing a suitable breed. Large, heavy dogs are not a good choice for multistory apartments, especially if the building lacks an elevator. For one thing, climbing a lot of stairs will harm the dog's joints over time. Further more, the dog might be injured someday and be unable to climb stairs at all. Consequently, the dog's body size and weight should be such that you can carry it without difficulties, should the need arise.

• If you rent, it is essential to find out before buying a puppy whether your lease allows you to keep a dog.

• Finally, let me point out that you will have to give up any "mania for neatness" if you become a dog owner. The truth is that dogs bring a lot of dirt into a house, not to mention the dog hairs that are flying around constantly, occasionally even making their way into your supper. This bothersome side of dog ownership is even worse with long-haired dogs and in shedding season.

Note: If, after careful consideration, you still are convinced that a dog is

the right pet for you, the rest of your family also has to be in agreement with the acquisition of a four-legged addition to the household. Never give a dog as a surprise gift; that can lead to undreamed-of quarrels and feuds.

Dogs and Children

It is an extremely positive experience for a child to have a dog as a playmate and companion. The child learns the right way to treat an animal; moreover, dealing with a pet promotes the development of a sense of responsibility and duty. Before you get your child a puppy, however, you need to consider these points:

• Proceed with care when choosing a breed. A "children's dog" should be sturdy and tolerant and not inclined to panicky or aggressive behavior.

• The dog needs to be given a chance to develop well. You, the parents, must see to that. In addition, you must provide food, attention, grooming, activity, and training. That would be simply too much to ask of any child.

• Don't get a puppy until your child is at least four years old. Small dogs can be quite wild when they play, and they may use their sharp little teeth to bite. They could be hurt by a very small child. Poor timing could cause very young children to become afraid of dogs.

It Must Be the Right Dog

After you've decided to add a dog to your family, a new question arises: How do we find the right dog? In order to live together in harmony, owner and dog must be a good match.

It is easiest to predict characteristics and needs with purebred dogs, because they are the result of carefully developed and maintained breeding programs. With mixed breeds, you can at least estimate their nature and appearance, assuming that you are certain which breeds are involved.

Before you decide on a certain breed, consider these two questions:
• What do you expect of your four-legged partner?
• What kind of life will it have in its new family?

Someone who likes to stay busy and spends a lot of time outdoors needs a different kind of dog than someone who is looking for a pet to share a quiet, less active life. Also to be considered is whether the dog will spend a great deal of time with people or will be used primarily as a watchdog. Are there children in your family, and what are their ages (see Dogs and Children, page 6)? The dog's appearance should be of lesser importance in your deliberations.

Many breeds need a very specific kind of activity and training in order to develop a healthy body and mind. These include the Border Collie, the Greyhound, the Husky, and several hunting dog breeds. If you are unable to offer such dogs the kind of life appropriate for the breed, serious behavioral problems frequently result. Other dog breeds are not suitable for novices but belong in the hands of people who have experience with dogs. In this category are the Kuvasz, the Doberman Pinscher, and the Rottweiler. The so-called fashionable dogs, on the other hand, often no longer possess the original characteristics of the breed and are usually more susceptible to disease.

Keep in mind that a sweet little puppy can grow into a large, imposing specimen.

After you make your choice, get as much information as possible before you make your purchase. For example, you can read other books (see page 62) or attend dog shows under the aegis of the American Kennel Club (AKC). Dates and locations of such shows are available directly from the AKC (see Addresses and Suggested Readings, page 62). At these shows, you can see relatively large numbers of representatives of most breeds. In addition, you can talk with breeders and other exhibitors.

My tip: For purchasing a purebred, it is best to go through the AKC. You will be given the addresses of reputable specialized breeders' associations for almost all breeds.

A Puppy or a Grown Dog?

The best preconditions for forging a close bond between dog and owner are present when you acquire a puppy. True, a puppy is more work than an older dog, but you will see your pet go through the most critical developmental phases of its life and have a chance

to guide and influence the process deliberately. The puppy will truly become your very own dog. With a full-grown dog, however, these phases are already in the past. If the development of such a dog left much to be desired, or if it has had bad experiences somewhere along the line, behavioral peculiarities could result, which may be very difficult or even impossible to correct. This applies especially to dogs that have had several owners or have grown up as wild or neglected animals.

Finding the Right Breeder

Whether you choose a purebred or a mongrel, the most important thing is for the dog to be raised by a good, reliable breeder. Because the first eight weeks are a decisive period of a dog's life, the breeder bears an enormous responsibility.

As a rule, a good breeder does not breed dogs to earn a living but rather is motivated by a love for dogs. He or she has a well-founded knowledge of canine behavior and genetics. In addition, a reputable breeder does not keep too many dogs and raises no more than one or two breeds.

The mother dog reprimands the puppy.

A further indication of a good breeder is the environment in which the puppies are raised. They should live in close contact with people, and they need ample opportunity to explore their surroundings, during outings at an "adventure playground," for example (see The Developmental Phases of Puppies, page 31).

Choosing Your Puppy

Not only do external conditions play a role in the choice of a puppy, but its physical state as well as the behavior of the mother dog and her litter of puppies are also important. All the animals should behave in a friendly, alert way and have a healthy appearance.

A healthy puppy has a glossy coat; clear, bright eyes; and a clean rear end. Sunken flanks, watering eyes, and a messy bottom are signs of disease. Caution is also called for if the bitch or her puppies seem anxious or fearful.

Don't buy if you don't get to see the mother dog, or if the "breeder" has only puppies, but no breeding dogs. In the final analysis, a purchase motivated by pity only lends support to unscrupulous dog dealers and puppy mills.

The pedigree provides information about the dog's lineage and identity. In it, you will find your puppy's ancestors on both sides, going back usually to its great-great-grandparents. To avoid the negative effects of inbreeding, your puppy's dam and sire should be unrelated, or only distantly related. If you are looking for a working dog—a hunting hound or a herd dog, for example—information about ancestors with appropriate qualifications will be recorded in the document, too. If championships and other titles are also present on the pedigree, that is a rea-

Tired from romping about, this little dog takes a short rest break.

sonable guarantee that the dog is a healthy, typical representative of its breed. It means that your puppy comes from a breeder who may belong to an association registered with the American Kennel Club, the national umbrella organization that includes most recognized special breed clubs. You also will see this abbreviation on pedigrees of famous show dogs, showing that they were bred in accordance with strict breeding standards.

Note: After you have found the right breeder, visit the puppies as often as possible. In that way, you will become familiar with their individual "personalities" and be able to choose the one that suits you best. In any event, our "puppy test" will help you make the correct choice (see pages 10–11).

HOW-TO:
Puppy Test

This test, developed by researcher William Campbell, will help you evaluate the litter and select the right puppy for you.

Both an ideal family pet and a working dog should be self-confident, yet responsive to your influence or training and willing to obey. Equally important is a

1 The puppy happily runs after the puppy tester.

well-developed ability to relate to humans. Dogs that are anxious and fearful or very dominant and aggressive are not recommended, particularly for "novice owners."

The puppy test will tell you about a puppy's tendencies toward dominance, anxiety, and insecurity and its ability to relate to humans. In addition to this fundamental disposition, the

puppy's subsequent development depends largely on the positive and negative experiences it has in the first year of life.

Running the Test

To obtain results as precise as possible, certain preconditions must be met.

• The puppies should be tested individually, at the end of the seventh week of life.

• The test area should be unfamiliar to the puppies. The best choice is an area measuring about 20 × 26 feet (6 × 8 m). A good substitute would be a fenced-in portion of lawn.

• During the test, the puppy should not be exposed to distractions of any kind. That means that onlookers, the breeder, the mother dog, and the puppy's littermates have to stay away from the test area.

• The tester should be someone the puppy does not know.

My tip: If you have already paid several visits to the puppies, let someone outside your circle of family and friends conduct the test, someone whom the dogs don't know.

The Test Situations
1. The Follow
Drawing 1

The puppy is behind the tester, who now walks away, as if by chance. If the tester must get the puppy's attention, he or she pats his or her own upper thigh.

Ideal Reaction

If the puppy immediately and cheerfully follows the tester, it

2 Relaxed, this puppy hangs loosely in the tester's hands.

has all the makings of a good family pet or utility dog.

Other Reactions

• A dominant puppy runs happily after the tester, but then jumps up on him or her and bites playfully at the tester.

• A willful or obstinate puppy goes its own way, unmoved by the tester's invitation.

• Anxious, mistrustful puppies may fail to follow, follow hesitantly, or slink away. The dog will cower, its tail tucked.

2. The Come
Drawing 4

Place the puppy in the middle of the testing area. The tester should quickly walk away from the puppy and then squat down and try to entice it to come closer by softly clapping his or her hands.

Ideal Reaction

The puppy, happily wagging its tail, immediately runs to the tester and licks his or her hands or offers a paw, displaying submissive behavior without a trace of fear.

Other Reactions
• A dominant puppy runs right to the tester, jumps up on him or her, and bites playfully.
• A willful puppy that does not relate well to humans shows no interest in the tester and goes its way, unaffected.
• An anxious, insecure puppy won't come at all, or follows only after long hesitation, creeping along or cringing, its tail tucked under all the way to its belly. Some actually are frozen with fear.

3. The Dangle
Drawing 2
The puppy is picked up from the back, below its shoulder blades, lifted a few inches off the ground, and held in this position for a minute.

Ideal Reaction
The puppy, unresisting and relaxed, puts up with everything.

Other Reactions
• A dominant puppy resists briefly, then stays calm and relaxed. It may try to bite playfully.
• A stubborn puppy that has trouble relating continues to struggle, growling and biting all the while.
• A mistrustful, insecure dog resists, becomes tense, and gets into a panic.
• A fearful dog stiffens its body, pulls its tail close to its belly, and trembles all over.

4. The Supine Position
Drawing 3
In this part of the test, the puppy is carefully placed on a soft pad, on its back, and held there with one hand on its chest.

Ideal Reaction
As with the dangle, the puppy submits, remaining calm and relaxed and offering no resistance.

Other Reactions
These reactions are similar to those described under Part 3.

5. Acoustic Stimulus
Put a mechanical alarm clock, a rubber squeak toy, or a similar object on the floor. As soon as the puppy approaches the object and looks at it, make whatever noise the object produces.

Ideal Reaction
The puppy is startled, runs a short distance away, comes back either on its own or in response to your enticements, and displays no fear.

Other Reactions
• A dominant puppy is only slightly startled, if at all, and

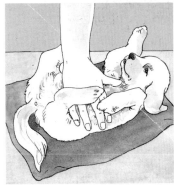

3 Unresisting, the puppy lets itself be placed on its back.

goes its way. It may try to pick up the object and carry it off.
• A willful puppy that has trouble relating is startled, runs away, and refuses to let itself be enticed to return.
• A mistrustful puppy comes back hesitantly, taking a roundabout way.
• A fearful puppy quivers and stiffens or possibly even flees, refusing to come back. Its manner of carrying itself clearly expresses fear.

4 In this test, the puppy is supposed to come when it hears a call and a handclap. Ideally, it will obey, with its tail wagging and with no sign of fear.

Making the Puppy Feel at Home

One day it will happen. The little dog will be old enough to leave its mother and littermates and move to its new home. Now you face the problem of finding the best way to transport the puppy to your house or apartment.

The Trip Home

By car: The car is probably the most common means of transportation. To keep the puppy from having unpleasant memories of the trip, keep these points in mind:

• Ideally, have someone accompany you. Then you can look after the puppy and let your companion drive. in this way, the little dog will establish close contact with you, its new master or mistress, from the very start.

• Equip yourself with a leash and collar, a blanket, and a roll of paper towels. Some puppies feel comfortable in a basket, lined with a blanket and placed on the floor in front of the passenger seat. Other puppies prefer to stay on your lap.

Important: Under no circumstances should you transport the puppy in a closed cardboard box or in the trunk of your car.

• To keep the little dog from getting sick to its stomach during the trip, don't let it eat anything for a period of several hours before your departure.

• If the trip home is lengthy, take water along and make several stops along the way, to let the dog relieve itself and get a little exercise. Be sure to put on its leash, to keep it from running away in panic if something frightens it.

You will want to consider an airline-type carrier if you and your pet will be

As if they knew that it's time to say goodbye, these two puppies are snuggling one last time.

making many car trips. After the important first trip home, a carrier is always the safest way for a pet to travel.

By plane: If you and the breeder live near an airport, flying is the shortest and easiest way to travel. If the puppy must make the trip home alone, an airline is the only way to go. Arrange to be able to pick up your new pet immediately upon arrival.

My tip: A few weeks ahead of time, ask the airline about the conditions of transport for four-legged passengers. If your puppy is coming from another country, ask the veterinarian or the local veterinary authorities in advance about the quarantine and any other restrictions that may govern the dog's entry.

The Puppy's Arrival in Its New Home

When you're back at home, immediately take the puppy to the place you've designated as its "potty area," and praise your new pet enthusiastically when it does its "business." If you teach it to use a patch of grass right away, it will look for the same place in the future and not be inclined to soil paths and sandboxes.

Next, lead or carry the little puppy into its new home, where it now can get acquainted with its new surroundings and its new "pack." Only family members should welcome the puppy the first day. Relatives and friends can meet the new addition later. The new "family" members, however, should not all pounce on the puppy at once. Instead, let the puppy initiate contact with each person.

The puppy may already be in the mood for a little game, and thus it will have a chance to try out its new toys right away. If it is hungry after the

A little dog needs plenty of attention and petting from its owner.

long trip, give it its first meal. Be sure to stay with the same puppy food your new pet has been eating. Set the food out in the place you've designated as the dog's eating area. A bowl of fresh water, too, should always be available there.

If the trip hasn't overtired the puppy, it now will want to explore its surroundings in detail. If it devotes too much attention to chair legs or carpet fringes or does anything else it's not supposed to, make it clear right from the start that some things are off limits. It would be a mistake to let the puppy do things during the first few days that will be forbidden from then on.

Before the puppy comes home, you need to have all its equipment ready and waiting.

Collar and Leash
Drawing 2

It is important for the leash and collar to be the right size for the puppy.

The leash should be adjustable in length. That is vital for later training sessions.

The collar should have an adjustable buckle so that it can be enlarged to fit the puppy as it grows. So-called double-chain "choke" collars are preferable for somewhat older puppies, especially those of large breeds, because the very limited restraint action allows you to have gentle control over your pet. Leather and cloth collars with a stop ring that causes

them to tighten slightly can fulfill the same purpose.

Unsuitable for puppies and young dogs are chains and other collars with unrestricted choke action. So-called automatically retractable leashes are not acceptable for training purposes. In addition, the dog may get in the habit of tugging at them. Chest harnesses, too, induce the dog to tug and can thus have a detrimental effect on the tendons and ligaments in its shoulder area, which are not yet very strong.

The Dog's Bed
Drawing 1

Two criteria are especially important in the choice of your pet's bed. First, it must be washable; second, the little puppy must feel comfortable in it. It must be soft and cuddly, and adequate in size. Young dogs usually prefer a cavelike bed. A wooden box lined with a blanket will do nicely.

1 In this pet carrier, the puppy can also go on trips.

An excellent suggestion is a crate, which looks like the carrier that is approved for air travel. It is closed on three sides, and the fourth side is equipped with a door made of metal grating. A crate gives your puppy its own "special place" in your home.

In addition there are those well-known willow baskets, even though they often fall victim to those sharp puppy teeth, and beds made of foam rubber with a washable cover. Also popular with dogs are cuddly floor cushions with plenty of stuffing; they, too, are equipped with washable fabric covers.

Bowls
Drawing 3

For its meals, the dog will need a food bowl and a water bowl. They are available in a variety of materials, including ceramics, stainless steel, and plastic. It is important that the bowls neither slide on the floor nor tip over. To keep the puppy

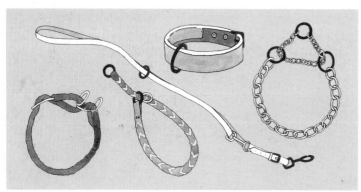

2 The adjustable leash ③ and leather collar ④ are used for walking a puppy. For a somewhat older dog, the best choices are cloth collars that tighten to a certain extent ① and ② or double-chain choke collars ⑤.

from tipping over the bowls they need to be large enough that the food and water fill only two thirds of their capacity. Bowls with extra-high sides for especially long-eared breeds such as hounds or spaniels will help keep ears out of the food.

The food, too, should already be on hand when the new family member moves in (see The Right Diet, page 20).

My tip: If at all possible, obtain the same food the breeder uses, to avoid changing the puppy's diet.

Grooming Equipment
Drawing 4

To groom the puppy's coat, you need—depending on the hair type and length—a brush, various combs, a soft natural-bristle brush, and a rubber brush for massage. Nail clippers are used to shorten overly long nails. A special moisturizing shampoo for dogs is good, should the little puppy get very dirty and need a bath (see Coat Care, page 23).

Toys

Because playing is extremely important for young dogs, it is vital that they have appropriate toys. It is best to keep special dog toys on hand for your puppy. Not only will they be safe for puppies, but your pet will also learn what it is allowed to play with and what it should leave alone. If you give the dog an old shoe, for example, it may later take one that is still wearable, since it can't see any difference between them.

Size: The toys should be appropriate for the puppy's size. Balls that are too small can easily be swallowed, and toys that are too big and heavy are hard to carry.

Material: In any case, a dog needs a ball that it can run after. Most suitable are standard solid rubber balls, as well as odd-shaped balls that reverse direction when they bounce. Balls that can be thrown long distances by means of a cord are not suitable for a puppy, because it is still too young to see that far.

Toys made of rawhide, such as bones, little cylinders, and other shapes, are good choices, both as playthings and as objects to gnaw on at length and to eat. Even Frisbees and boomerangs made of rawhide are available.

Dogs also love games that involve pulling and tugging. Ideal for this purpose are solid rubber rings and "knots" made

3 The bowls must be skidproof and hard to knock over.

of heavy rope. For summer fun in the water, there are special throwing rings that float.

Many dogs like toys that squeak. Here you have a wide choice, ranging from hedgehogs to rubber pork chops.

Note: Don't throw small sticks to your puppy. It can be seriously injured if the stick lodges in its throat when it is trying to make the catch.

4 Grooming utensils, depending on hair length, include a soft natural-bristle brush ①, a fine-toothed/broad-toothed comb ②, a glove with rubber nubs ④, various combs ⑤ and ⑥, and nail clippers for nail care ③.

"Who's stronger?" is a game that can be played in all situations in life.

Bed: If the little dog is very tired after the trip home and wants to sleep, you should show the puppy its bed. If the breeder gave you a blanket or something else that smells of its mother and littermates, put it in the puppy's bed. Your pet may immediately accept its designated place at once, or it may need your tender encouragement to do so. The little puppy needs to be left undisturbed now. When it has had enough rest, it will initiate contact on its own.

My tip: The family member who will bear primary responsibility for your pet's initial training and possibly will attend obedience courses with it later on should spend a great deal of time with the puppy now, during the first few days. That will create a close bond between the puppy and it key person from the very outset. This is an important precondition for good cooperation later on.

Housebreaking Your Pet

First, the puppy must be housebroken. If you set aside enough time for this task, the dog will quickly know what you expect of it. Take the puppy outdoors—to the same spot each time—after every meal, every time it wakes up, and after every play session. The scent of its own urine and feces in that spot will act as a stimulus, causing it to relieve itself. Praise the puppy lavishly whenever it is "successful." Keep a close eye on it at other times as well, however. Sniffing the ground excitedly and turning around in a circle are signs that the dog has to go. When you see either behavior, carry your pet outdoors quickly. While it does its business, always be liberal in your praise. If you want to use a training phrase like "Let's go outside," your puppy may learn to relieve itself more or less on command. This can be very useful, for example, on trips or when you don't have time for a lengthy walk.

To keep the puppy dry through the night, don't let it have anything more to drink from late afternoon on. Because a dog does not like to soil its bed, its radius of action should be kept very small. If you don't use a sleeping crate (which is always best), you can resort to a little trick. Put the puppy's bed in a box that it can't climb out of, or fence in a small area surrounding its bed with boards or the like.

Note: Under no circumstances should you tie the puppy up to limit its sphere of movement, for example. It could get tangled in the leash and strangle. In addition, it must see the leash from a very unpleasant vantage point.

If the little dog ever has an accident in your home, don't scold it. It could link the punishment with the activity itself, rather than with the choice of the wrong place. At worst, it might—out of fear of a punishment it doesn't comprehend—no longer dare to do its "business" in the presence of human beings. Disinfect and deodorize the spot thoroughly, to keep the scent from lingering and acting as a stimulus and leading the puppy to "go" there again.

Things become difficult if you live in a high-rise apartment building and can't always get to a patch of grass quickly enough to set the dog down on it. Then it is advisable to get the puppy used to a little box for the time being. If you line it with grass or the like, the dog will have an easier time adjusting to a natural surface later on. This is only a substitute for the "special" spot outside.

Getting Used to the Collar and Leash

To get the little dog used to its collar, put it on your pet indoors, too, not only when you go out for walks. To make this a positive experience, draw a connection between wearing the collar and pleasant situations. Let the puppy wear the collar while it eats, for example, or as it plays. The collar should fit the dog's neck loosely, but without allowing the puppy to slip it off. To accustom the puppy to its leash, proceed in a similar fashion. If your pet resists, let it lead you at first. Go in the direction it chooses, if possible. You can take a toy along as well and play with your dog, on its leash, or romp around with it.

It should not view the leash as a plaything, however, and start to gnaw on it (see Leash Training, page 54).

HOW-TO:
Eliminating Hazards

Young dogs are extremely curious and want to investigate and test everything thoroughly. Frequently, however, they are unable to assess the hazards of our civilized environment correctly. For this reason, it is important to check out your home and yard to see whether they are "puppy proof," in order to prevent injuries or worse.

1 Cover polished or slippery floors with carpeting, to keep the puppy from losing its footing.

Gnawing and Eating
Drawing 4

Some little dogs are content with rather superficial explorations of your home, where as nothing is safe with other puppies. Everything that is lying out is chewed on and swallowed, if possible, including toy figures, building blocks, broken bits and pieces, nails, or sewing needles. Also injurious to health are eating pieces of carpet or carpet fringe; licking at detergent, cleaning agents, and chemicals; and nibbling on poisonous house plants. The dog will try electric cables and wall sockets to see how they taste or will see what happens when it pulls on the tablecloth.

All these everyday things can lead to serious injuries or even to death.

Remedial action: Keep things picked up, don't leave dangerous objects lying around, and don't keep poisonous plants in your home and yard (see Yard, page 19). Store chemicals and cleaning agents securely in cupboards and cover wall plugs with the childproof caps available in electrical goods stores. Don't leave unconcealed wires and cables live; instead, pull the plugs when you leave the house. Above all, keep a close eye on the puppy, just as if it were a human toddler.

Floors
Drawing 1

Puppies are not as steady on their legs as grown dogs. Consequently, very smooth or polished floor surfaces often are fairly unpleasant for them. A little puppy's legs slip out from under it, and it suddenly is flat on the ground. Because the tendons and ligaments are still very soft at this age, frequent slipping can harm your pet's health. Especially at risk are puppies of large, heavy breeds.

Remedial action: The best solution is to cover the areas where the dog spends most of its time with carpets or mats. Under your loving supervision, however, the puppy should become acquainted with polished floors early on, so that it won't develop feelings of insecurity and anxiety later.

Stairs
Drawing 3

On smooth stone or wooden stairs, too, a little puppy can easily lose its footing and come to harm. If the steps are carpeted, the danger is lessened.

Remedial action: Make it a rule that the puppy does not use any stairs unsupervised. Under your watchful eye, however, start now to get your pet used to stairs of different types, to prevent anxiety later. To avoid accidents, install safety gates of the kind used for small children.

Windows and Balconies

The puppy could fall out of a window that can be reached by a chair or a couch, for example, or fall off a balcony with bars

2 A cellar stairwell should be enclosed.

3 Gates are a good safety device for stairs.

Poisonous Plants

Check your garden for poisonous plants, such as foxglove, laburnum, autumn crocus, ligustrum, lilies of the valley, rhododendron, and others (look in a book on plants or contact your local county agent). Especially tempting for dogs are the fruits of these plants.

Remedial action: Remove the plants or find a way to keep the puppy from getting at them.

Pool or Pond

If the pool or pond has sufficiently large, very flat banks, there is really no great danger for the puppy. In ponds with steep sides, however, a young dog can easily drown because it can't get out unaided.

Remedial action: Surround the swimming pools with a fence. That is a good idea in any case because few pools benefit from being used as dog baths.

Basement Access Stairs and Recesses in the Floor
Drawing 2

A puppy can fall into unsecured basement access stairwells or step into any floor recesses and possibly become injured.

Remedial action: Fence in stairwells temporarily. Fill in or cover any recesses that are no longer in use or are seldom used.

Gardening Tools and Bicycles

Because as mentioned previously, nothing is safe from

4 Wall sockets should be covered and electric cords removed.

that the little dog can squeeze through.

Remedial action: Don't leave windows open, and secure your balcony with a net or a fine-mesh grating.

Yard

In the yard, too, all kinds of dangers await your puppy. In any case, your property should be completely fenced. Depending on the type of fence and the puppy's size, it may be a good idea to put up a fine-mesh wire fence in addition, to keep the little rascal from gaining its freedom.

Even with an "escapeproof" yard, however, the puppy shouldn't necessarily be left alone outdoors. Not everyone is a dog lover, unfortunately, and many a dog has been found poisoned or has suddenly disappeared from the property.

some puppies, you need to make sheds in which gardening tools and/or bikes are stored, inaccessible to your dog. It can get hurt by many kinds of yard tools. Bicycles can fall over and land on top of it.

Note: These are a few examples of things and situations that could place your puppy in danger. It is entirely possible, however, that there are other objects in your house or yard that are dangerous for a young dog. Consequently, you need to keep an eye on the little animal at all times and watch closely to see what catches its special interest. One of the best ways to do this is to get down on all fours, at "puppy-eye level" and scan your environment for sharp corners, unsafe places, and other things that can injure an inquisitive and innocent young puppy.

The Right Diet

Special importance should be attached to a proper diet during puppyhood and adolescence. Keep in mind that most dog breeds, including the large ones, have attained their final height at shoulder level by the end of their first year of life. Thus you can imagine what your pet's system needs to accomplish during this period.

The Basics of Feeding

If you bought your four-legged friend from an experienced, reputable breeder, you can assume that the puppy was fed an excellent diet there.

Keep to this diet after the puppy has joined your household, to avoid placing additional stress on your pet. Only then, if absolutely necessary, should you begin to gradually change its diet.

My tip: If you aren't quite sure whether your puppy's previous diet was ideal, have the breeder tell you in detail what foods the dog was given, and convey this information to your veterinarian, who will be able to advise you.

Four meals a day at the start: A young dog usually consumes proportionally more than a grown member of the species. Because a puppy, in contrast to a full-grown dog, still has a more sensitive digestive system, you must spread the daily ration over several feedings. That is, until the age of about six months, your pet should have four meals a day: in the morning after its first outing, at midday, in the afternoon, and in the evening.

Don't feed the puppy human food. High-quality commercial puppy foods are best. They contain everything the puppy needs and are completely balanced. If you follow the breeder's or veterinarian's instructions exactly when preparing your puppy's food, you won't go wrong.

The older the dog, the fewer the meals: When your dog is about six months old, reduce the number of feedings to three: morning, midday, and evening. By the age of approximately nine months, the dog needs only two daily feedings, and one meal a day is enough for a one-year-old dog.

Daily ration divided in half: Many dogs, however, do better if their daily ration is spread out over two meals even after they have reached "adulthood." Make the breakfast serving slightly smaller, and serve the larger main meal in the early evening. In general, dogs are "creatures of habit," and they always expect their food to be served at roughly the same time and in the same place.

Rest after meals: After your four-legged pet has eaten, it needs to stay fairly quiet for one or two hours; otherwise, there is a risk of gastric torsion. Most young dogs lie down voluntarily for a little rest after meals. However, if you have an active puppy that wants

After eating, a young dog needs to rest.

Puppies enjoy chewing on almost anything.

you to play again right away, you should refuse to participate.

The Right Amount

Determining the right amount is an important aspect of proper nutrition for a young dog. There is often great uncertainty here. Although a puppy needs plenty of energy for its development, you should under no circumstances overfeed it. Its joints and ligaments are still very soft at this stage, and overweight would place unnecessary stress on them. Excess poundage would also impair the young dog's vitality and mobility. Here are a few guidelines for determining the right amount of food:

• Until the age of four to five months, a little puppy fat is just fine. You should always be able to feel your pet's ribs easily under its coat, however.
• A young dog ought to be hungry before every meal and finish its food within the space of a few minutes. If it leaves some in the bowl, the serving was too large. Keep that in mind at the next meal.
• Young dogs that are already undergoing training or play a lot with other dogs need more food than those who lead a quieter existence.

Dry and Canned Foods

There are many advantages to using high-quality commercial dog foods.

They contain all the nutrients puppies and growing dogs need, in the ideal composition. In addition, they save time, are easy to prepare, and can be carried along everywhere without difficulty.

A great many varieties of ready-to-serve foods are available. You can choose among complete foods, basic foods, and supplementary foods. All three types are available in formulas designed especially for puppies and young dogs (see package labeling).

• Complete foods contain all the dog's needs; there is no need for supplements.

• The better the puppy food you use, the better the nutritional outcome you can expect.

Nutritionally complete foods are available in both dry and canned forms.

• Dry food contains meat and grain products, as well as all the necessary vitamins and minerals. Because of the reduced water content—only about 10 to 20 percent water—this type of food is far higher in energy than the canned variety. You can either serve it as is to your pet or add warm water or broth to make a mush. Dry products are usually the most economical and best overall choice.

Note: If you use dry food, your dog always must have fresh water available so that it can drink a lot.

• Nutritionally complete canned food also consists of meat, vegetables, and cereal, along with vitamins and minerals. It contains about 80 percent moisture, which means that the nutrients are less concentrated than in the dry food. Stools also tend to be looser when a pet is fed a 100 percent canned food diet.

• In addition, stores offer a wide range of treats and dog biscuits for between meals and rewards.

Information on portion size is provided on package labels. Nevertheless, you need to pay attention to your little dog's weight and its behavior at mealtime. Not all dogs metabolize their food the same way, so you may need to reduce or increase the quantities recommended.

The brand you choose depends first on your pet's tolerance for each type of food and second on its taste. Find a good dog food (probably the one the breeder was using), one that suits your dog's taste and meets all the other requirements and stick with it. Dogs don't need constant variety; on the contrary, that would only place a needless burden on their digestive systems. Avoid table scraps and all human foods because these will upset the complete balance of the commercial puppy food. Feeding table food also leads to an annoying habit—begging.

Home-Prepared Foods

One hears a lot of discussion about homemade pet diets. Some of this talk comes from Europe where the top brands of dog food are just becoming established and pet owners have had years of having to make-do. Consequently, this attitude has become ingrained in some people's minds. The best advice a new puppy owner can get is to use the food the breeder was using and stay with it if at all possible. If a change is necessary that change should be undertaken only after much study and then on a very gradual timetable.

Unless you are, or are willing to become, a trained animal nutritionist, leave the development of your pet's food to the experts. The top dog food makers in the United States have developed their products over decades of intensive research and at a cost of many millions of dollars. These foods are recognized as nutritionally excellent by dog breeders and veterinarians at every level.

Even though it is theoretically possible that you could develop a food of equal quality with America's best commercial brands, why should you? Unless you are absolutely certain about how much protein, carbohydrates, and fats would be in any food you would make, you would be gambling with your dog's nutritional well-being. It is quite easy to over- or undersupplement a diet with vitamins and minerals. Is this a chance you are willing to take?

Feeding your pet doesn't need to be a passive undertaking. You can study different brands. Read some of the available research on nutrition, and discover which foods are best for your dog as it goes through the various phases of its life. You and your dog would be far better off if you turned your dietetic interests to knowing which reputable brand to offer than trying to concoct something of your own.

How Much Food?

In conclusion, here are a few additional guidelines for determining how much food to serve your pet:

Small breeds, 12 weeks old: Four meals each day, based on breeder or veterinarian recommendations as to actual amount.

Medium-sized breeds, 12 weeks old: Four meals each day, based on breeder or veterinarian recommendations as to the actual amount.

Large breeds, 12 weeks old: Four meals each day, based on breeder or

To rest and sleep, a little dog may like to snuggle on a soft floor cushion. It should have abundant stuffing and a washable cover.

veterinarian recommendations as to actual amount.

Note: Because there are great differences from breed to breed and even within breeds, these amounts are only rough indications. For more detailed information, contact your pet's breed club or, even better, your veterinarian, who is acquainted with your dog on a "personal" basis.

Regular Grooming

Besides a proper diet, your puppy needs regular grooming if it is to feel happy and stay healthy overall. It is advisable to accustom the dog as early as possible to having its coat groomed, its teeth and nails checked, and its ears cleaned. True, these procedures are not so crucial for a puppy as for a full-grown dog, but your pet needs to become familiar with them so that it will enjoy the grooming routine later on, rather than find it unpleasant.

Coat Care

A wide range of different combs and brushes is available for coat care. Your four-legged friend's coat type will determine which "tools" are right. It is important to proceed carefully and gently when combing and brushing the coat, to keep from hurting the puppy. Finally, the daily grooming routine should always be a

Negotiating stairs is a little adventure for a puppy.

pleasant experience for the dog, not a source of unpleasant associations.

Short- and thick-haired dogs are the easiest to groom. For short-haired breeds such as Dalmatians, use a soft natural-bristle brush. Thick-haired dogs such as Labradors are groomed with a brush that has short, wide metal teeth.

First, brush against the lie of the hair. Then, for both hair types, brush in the direction of the coat's growth—that is, from front to back—using a rubber brush, also available as a grooming glove. That will give the coat a slight gloss as well.

Medium- and long-haired breeds such as setters or Newfoundlands and **curly-haired dogs** such as poodles need very careful grooming because their coats mat easily. It is advisable to give these breeds a preliminary combing with a so-called dematting comb. Next, use a medium-fine comb on the coat. Long-haired dogs, too, enjoy a final massage with the rubber grooming glove.
Note: Some dog breeds, such as poodles or many of the terrier breeds, must be trimmed regularly. It is best to take your pet to a dog grooming salon unless you have the time and money to learn grooming yourself.

Bathing

For "normal" dirtiness, rinsing your dog off in the tub or shower with lukewarm water is sufficient. In conclusion, towel it thoroughly dry. This is especially important with a puppy, because its "baby hair" insulates less well than the coat of an older dog.

Using bath additives is normally unnecessary and should be avoided, to protect skin and hair. It's another matter, however, if your four-legged friend has rolled in manure or the like. Here, it is essential to use a shampoo formulated for dogs, a product that is pH neutral and contains special moisturizing agents (available in pet stores). Then the puppy's coat will regain its natural protection against cold and damp, and, in addition, the skin's acidproof coating will be largely preserved. Don't bathe your pet too often or its skin and coat will suffer.

Dental Care

A proper diet is an important factor in keeping your puppy's teeth healthy. If the dog is given no sweets or other leftovers from your table but is fed only what is appropriate for its species, dental problems are unlikely to occur.

Hard dog biscuits do a good job of helping to clean teeth. Rawhide bones, strips of hide, and the like fulfill much the same purpose. A young dog needs plenty to chew and gnaw, particularly when it gets its second set of teeth, starting in about the fourth month of life.
Note: When the puppy is cutting its new teeth, make sure that the milk teeth fall out. If the new tooth has fully erupted and the milk tooth is still present, the veterinarian will have to remove it.

Nail Care

In a grown dog that spends a lot of time outdoors and frequently runs on asphalt-covered surfaces, the nails usually need no special care. Puppies and young dogs are out and about less often, however; they still spend much of their time indoors. It may happen that your pet's nails become too long. Their length is right if, when the dog is standing, they just fail to touch the ground.

Overly long nails are trimmed with special nail clippers. As you clip, make sure that you don't injure a blood vessel. If the nails are light in color, the blood vessels frequently are easily visible; with dark nails, however, it is better to trim only a little. If you are very unsure of yourself, the veterinarian will do this for you. Pay special attention to the so-called dewclaws, or vestigial claws, if any are present. They are located between the heel and the paw on the insides of the hind legs, and if they grow too long, they can grow abnormally into the flesh.

An "adventure playground" where puppies can nose around and dig.

Eye and Ear Care

Eyes: Healthy eyes normally need no special care. Only if excessive matter has collected in the dog's eyes should you wipe it out with a soft, lint-free dry or dampened cloth. This is especially important for dogs with breed-related problems, such as the Pug and the Basset Hound. Also some

Puppies need plenty of things to chew, like this shoe made of rawhide.

slight amount of mucuslike matter may appear in the corner of the eyes. This is normal and can be simply wiped away. Excessive eye matter indicates a problem.

Note: To prevent conjunctivitis, never let your dog stick its head out of the window while riding in a car.

Ears: The ears, too, must be checked regularly. Dogs with drooping ears are particularly susceptible to ear diseases, because air can't circulate well in their auditory passages.

Approximately every two weeks, clean the outer ear with a cotton ball or soft cloth soaked in baby or mineral oil. In addition, you can put a few squirts of an ear-cleaning solution in each ear. These ear-care products are available in pet stores and from your veterinarian.

Note: Because of the danger of injury, never clean the inner ear, and never, under any circumstances, insert a cotton swab or the like into the ear.

Other Grooming Procedures

Some dogs, especially as they grow older, have a tendency to develop calluses on their elbows, sometimes on their heels as well. To keep the skin in such areas from cracking and becoming inflamed, rub it regularly with petroleum jelly. That is especially important in winter, when the dog walks on sidewalks sprinkled with thawing salt. In pet stores, protective sprays are available for this purpose. In winter, they also prevent clumps of snow from building up on the feet of long-haired dogs. Giving an older dog a cushion or mat to lie down on will also help to prevent calluses.

Preventive Health Care

Along with good nutrition and excellent grooming, vaccinations and worm treatments are also essential requirements for the health of a young dog. Because several infectious diseases as well as some worms are communicable to humans, special attention has to be paid to this aspect of health care. Nevertheless, your puppy may become ill. To detect signs that something is wrong in time, you need to keep a close eye on your young dog.

Is Your Puppy Healthy?

Both the appearance and the behavior of your young puppy will provide information about the state of its health. When it's not sleeping, a healthy young dog is lively and interested in everything, likes to play, eats well, and makes an overall impression of contentment.

Here are a few things to look for in your dog's appearance:
• The coat is glossy and soft.
• The anal area is clean, not messy or soiled.

• The ears, eyes, and nose are neither sticky nor festering.
• The mucous membranes and gums are pink.
• Because of its baby fat, the puppy looks slightly chubby.

Vaccinations

Vaccinations at regular intervals protect the dog against a number of dangerous infectious diseases: distemper, canine hepatitis, kennel cough, parvovirus disease, rabies, and leptospirosis.

The last two are also communicable to humans. If an unvaccinated dog contracts rabies, distemper, parvovirus disease, or hepatitis, that is usually a death sentence for the animal. Kennel cough and leptospirosis can be treated, but the dog still should be vaccinated against them.

A rabies vaccination is compulsory. If you want your pet to participate in events such as dog shows, trials, or training courses, you must show proof of vaccination for rabies. The same is especially true if you intend to travel abroad.

The table on page 30 tells when the puppy should be vaccinated and against which diseases.

My tip: When you buy a puppy, make sure the appropriate vaccinations for its age are listed on the vaccination certificate. If you have doubts, take the puppy to your veterinarian as soon as you get it.

Worming

Regular worming is essential. A dog afflicted with worms is weakened and thus more susceptible to diseases. In addition, some worm species are communicable to humans. Children in particular are at risk.

Puppies get their first worms—ascarids, or intestinal worms—while they are still inside their mother's body. Thus they need to be wormed at these ages:
• six weeks
• eight weeks
• twelve weeks
• six months
• nine months

These first two worm treatments are the breeder's responsibility.

A grown dog should be wormed twice a year. Worming or worming preparations are available from your veterinarian.

Note: To ensure that your dog is healthy, when a vaccination is scheduled have your veterinarian check for worms.

Additional worm treatments are necessary if the dog has fleas or frequently digs for mice and possibly eats them. Fleas and mice are intermediate hosts of the canine tapeworm, which is also communicable to humans. Apart from ascarids and tapeworms, a dog also can get hookworms, whipworms, and lungworms, as well as coccidia (parasitic protozoa).

Familiarize your dog with water while it is still a puppy.

If the infestation is severe, eggs, larvae, or worms—depending on the species—will be visible in the dog's stool. The coccidia can be seen only through a microscope.

Heartworms: In many places in the United States, heartworms, transmitted by the bite of a particular mosquito, will affect dogs. Puppies will need heart worm preventatives after they reach a certain age. Your veterinarian can advise you on this and supply the appropriate preventative.

Treatment for Skin Parasites

Among the parasites that can infest a dog's skin are ticks, lice, bird lice, fleas, and mites. The consequences may include eczema and hair loss. Ticks are transmitters of borreliosis (often called Lyme Disease), whereas fleas transmit tapeworms. Borreliosis is a bacterial infection of the joints and skin that results in chronic problems. It is also communicable to humans. To protect yourself and your dog against these unpleasant visitors, you should check its coat and skin regularly. Depending on the type of parasite, you may find excrement or eggs in the dog's coat. Mites leave a rust-brown deposit on a dog's skin, especially in the ears. In addition, your pet will scratch itself very noticeably.

Ticks bore into the skin and suck themselves full of blood. They range from pinhead-size to pea-size, and they can be removed with special tick tweezers without any difficulty. Infestation with the other parasites, however, calls for a trip to the veterinarian. **Note:** In a case of flea infestation, it is important, moreover, that not only the dog but also its surroundings be treated as well, since that is where most of the fleas will be found.

With vaccinations, the most dangerous infectious diseases can be prevented. Full protection is ensured, however, only if the dog receives boosters at certain intervals.

The Sick Puppy

Digestive System: In puppies and young dogs, the digestive system is frequently somewhat sensitive, particularly if the dog comes from a kennel that is less than spotless. If your puppy refuses to eat and if it has diarrhea in addition, a trip to the veterinarian is definitely in order. The same is true if there is frequent vomiting. Because of the great loss of fluids that goes along with severe vomiting and diarrhea, the little dog is in danger of becoming severely dehydrated.

If your pet is under six months old and begins to show evidence of these symptoms, don't wait around hoping for improvement, it must see the veterinarian.

Movement Problems: If your dog is limping, that is a primary indication of a problem with its muscle or skeletal system. If the affected foot shows no sign of injury, your little dog may have sprained its leg or pulled a muscle. It may also be attributable to a temporary tenderness caused by growing pains. It is best for the dog to take things easy for several days. If the lameness persists or recurs, the puppy must see the veterinarian. Similarly, take your pet to the veterinarian if it has trouble getting on its feet or cries out in pain when making certain movements.

Unfortunately there are a few serious diseases, some of them genetic in origin, that require extensive treatment. These include, for example, canine hip dysplasia (CHD), a malformation of the head of the femur and the hip socket. Limping may also be caused by osteochondrosis. With this disease, bone splinters develop during the growth phase. In large, fast-growing breeds, bone curvatures can be the result. Additional causes of limping are torn ligaments and dislocated kneecaps.

Nothing is more exciting for a puppy than exploring its surroundings step by step.

Vaccination Schedule for Preventive Care

Active against	Basic Immunization		Reinoculations	Boosters
	Sixth to eighth weeks	Eighth to tenth weeks	Eleventh to fourteenth weeks	Twelve months after basic immunization
Parvovirus disease*	+		+	+annually
Kennel cough	+		+	+annually
Hepatitis*		+	+	+at least every two years
Leptospirosis*		+	+	+annually
Distemper*		+	+	+at least every two years
Rabies*		+	+	+annually

*Note: Another possibility is annual inoculation with multiple (five) vaccines, recommended especially in areas with a high incidence of distemper or hepatitis.

Sensory Organs and Skin: Go to the veterinarian if your pet's eyes weep continually, if its eyelids are stuck together, or if the conjunctiva is reddened. If your dog holds its head at a tilt and scratches at its ear frequently, an ear disease is indicated. Often you will also find a dark, foul-smelling deposit in the auditory canal.

Symptoms of skin diseases, which also can occur in dogs, are bare, often inflamed patches in the coat, rashes, and frequent scratching. The causes can include allergies, skin fungi, and parasitic infestation. In any event, a trip to the veterinarian is necessary.

Note: This book has space only for a brief overview of possible diseases. Consequently, you always should consult the veterinarian if you observe unusual changes in your dog's behavior or appearance.

The Developmental Phases of Puppies

The next section in this book deals with a very important aspect of your pet's life: its psychological and physical development; that is, the development of the dog's inner nature and physical abilities in the first six months of its existence.

The dog is a teachable animal. At first, its actions still are guided predominantly by innate behavior, but soon the environment, with a host of impressions and stimuli, influences the puppy's development to an increasing extent. That is, the experiences the dog has with its environment and the lessons it learns from those experiences largely determine the effect of its innate characteristics. Thus, in the final analysis, it is the interaction of inherent and learned factors that shapes our pet's nature.

An additional important aspect is the great responsibility that both the breeder and the future owner bear for the puppy's healthy development. You will learn just what that entails here.

The First Three Weeks

After a gestation period of roughly 63 days, a puppy is born. Its eyes and ears are still closed, and the little dog appears quite helpless and somewhat incomplete. Nonetheless, it is full of vitality. Within its immediate surroundings, its sense of smell and its perception of varying degrees of heat are already functioning.

The most important thing for the puppy in these first few weeks is the satisfaction of its vital needs for nourishment and the warmth and shelter of a nest. Equally critical to its further development is the emergence of what is known as basic trust. This is communicated to the puppy through its mother's loving nurture and care, assuming she has normal inclinations and demonstrates characteristic "brood care behavior" by hovering constantly over her young.

First learning achievement: After its mother has removed its umbilical cord and licked its little body all over, the puppy, now ready for its life to begin, will expend all its energy to find her teats, using its sense of smell, and to secure a nipple for itself. Apart from

Puppies press very close together to sleep. In this way, they satisfy their need for warmth, security, and trust.

Patiently this female Fox Terrier waits for each puppy to have its "turn."

the fact that its mother's milk is a vital necessity, reaching the teats on its own has yet another meaning.

The puppy has learned its first lesson: It has succeeded through its own efforts and has achieved a pleasant state—the cessation of hunger. Naturally, searching for the teats and holding its own against its littermates entails a certain amount of stress for a puppy. Behavioral scientists, however, have found that this stress is quite important, even essential, to a dog's healthy development.

Second learning achievement: It is the same thing as far as physical contact is concerned. Puppies have the habit of pressing very close together to sleep or of snuggling close to their mother. In this way, they satisfy their need for vital warmth, security, and trust. Every puppy, using its capacity to perceive temperature, does its utmost to find the warmest place in the group.

Here, too, the puppy succeeds through its own efforts, under some degree of stress, and finally achieves a pleasant, satisfied feeling. This is yet another important experience that promotes the healthy development of its ability to learn and feel rewarded for its efforts.

Unnatural Conditions

Unfortunately, some puppies are too weak or sick after birth to survive without help. Instinctively, their mothers recognize such puppies and usually refuse to take care of them. In the wild, they soon would die. This process of natural selection is a way of ensuring that only strong, fit animals grow to maturity and later reproduce.

With domestic dogs, however, owners often choose to nurse these weak puppies, which in fact are nonviable, to keep them alive. They are fed without having to make much effort, and—if they can't stay with their littermates—they usually are kept warm by artificial sources of heat, which create an area of such even warmth that the puppy really doesn't care which portion it occupies.

These unnatural conditions deprive such young dogs of their most important early learning experiences. Moreover, they are also spared the stress to which healthy puppies are exposed in their search for physical contact and their mother's teats. At first glance, this may seem advantageous for the puppies concerned, since in the absence of strain and exertion they can catch up to their littermates and sometimes even overtake them.

The truth is just the opposite, however. Results of behavioral research indicate that the absence of these natural conditions in the early phase of the puppy's life can lead to a host of behavioral problems later because important developmental processes have been interrupted or omitted entirely.

The Third Week of Life

At approximately the beginning of the third week, the puppy reaches an important milestone. Its eyes open, and its hearing begins to function. Its milk teeth, too, come in. These changes allow its faculty of perception to increase, and the little dog's desire to move about increases as well. Now it begins to explore its surroundings actively, and it is equipped for the next, extremely decisive period of its life.

Significance for the Dog Owner

The significance of these factors for the future owner of a puppy depends primarily on what he or she intends to do with the dog. Secondarily, the breed has a certain role to play. Basically, it is important for every young dog to have a loving, nurturing mother and to grow up in the best possible conditions.

Training: If, however, you intend to train the dog for a certain purpose—for example, as a hunting dog, a rescue dog, or a seeing-eye dog—you need to make sure that the puppy has grown up in as natural a way as possible, to avoid problems later on. Puppies of utility breeds, particularly those bred from a performance-oriented line, usually are subject to stronger impulses than pure lap dogs or companion dogs. Hence an unnatural rearing can have more intense effects on them.

Breeding: If you want to breed your dog later, you need to be especially careful when choosing a puppy. In this case, you should look for a thoroughly lively, completely fit puppy. In this way you can help prevent defects, which impair a dog's fitness for life, from being passed on to subsequent generations.

How do you taste? The little Basset has to be taught early that it mustn't nibble at a turtle.

The Imprinting Phase

The imprinting or bonding phase begins at the start of the fourth week of life and lasts until about the beginning of the eighth week. After the puppy's eyes and ears are open, the world is open to it, so to speak. Step by step the little dog's radius of action is enlarging. At the same time, its mind and body are developing in complementary fashion.

Indelible Experiences

The more active and mobile the puppy is, the more eagerly it will explore its surroundings. Nature has decreed that a puppy's brain, in accordance with its age, is receptive to certain stimuli and experiences for certain lengths of time. Whatever the puppy learns in these phases is imprinted almost indelibly in its brain.

Among undomesticated canines, nature guarantees that the puppies are exposed to the stimuli in their environ-ment that are appropriate to their stage of development. Thus everything essential for their survival in the wild can become imprinted in their brain.

Domestic dogs grow up under very different conditions, and it is up to humans to "supply" puppies with the appropriate stimuli, to equip them for "survival" in our civilized world. Whatever is missed during these phases often is difficult, if not impossible, to make up for later.

Imprinting on other dogs: Imprinting on other dogs is one of the most important processes in the imprinting phase. When, at the beginning of this developmental stage, all the senses begin to operate, the puppy for the first time is able to see, hear, and smell its mother and siblings. The image produced by these impression is lastingly imprinted in the young dog's brain.

Imprinting on humans: Imprinting on humans occurs between the third and eighth weeks and is necessary if the dog is to view humans, too, as fellow members of its species in the larger sense. This imprinting, which is a prerequisite for the best possible relationship of trust between dog and human, is possible only within this span of time; it cannot be made up for later. During this time, puppies need close contact with different people, in order to accumulate many good experiences. Visitors should pet them, pick them up, and play with them. For a future family pet, it is ideal to be able to have good experiences with children at this time. A dog that has little

Children and puppies make good comrades, provided that the child has learned how a puppy should be treated.

or no contact with people at this stage can, depending on its character, become accustomed to them to a certain extent. However, it will never be as trusting and receptive to contact as an imprinted dog. Often, an animal of this kind is never totally reliable in its dealings with humans, and in the worst case it can turn into a dog that bites out of fear.

Imprinting on other pets: Imprinting on other pets also is possible at this stage. If the puppy grows up with "dog-friendly" cats, it will get along well with them later on, too.

A Greater Range of Action

In terms of physical development, the puppy also makes great progress at this stage of life.

In the period after birth, the puppy could propel itself forward only by creeping or crawling. Now it learns other methods of locomotion, including climbing, jumping, and running. Naturally, it still is quite unsteady and clumsy. But it is physically and mentally advanced enough to leave its cozy shelter and explore the immediate surroundings. Its range of action continues to expand.

To develop properly, the puppy needs an opportunity to gather a great many experiences through interaction with its environment. Everything it becomes acquainted with now will be natural and self-evident for it later on. If the puppy grows up indoors, it automatically encounters everything that is part of everyday life, such as a vacuum cleaner, a mixer, and various types of floor coverings. A responsible breeder will provide his or her puppies with a kind of "adventure playground" with a variety of possible activities and games. Some breeders take little outings with the

The younger cats and dogs are when they become acquainted, the better they will get along together.

mother dog and her puppies just to explore things, or they take them out in the car a few times. From this standpoint, puppies born in spring or summer sometimes have far more opportunities to explore their environment than those born in fall or winter.

Social Behavior

The puppy learns something else during the imprinting phase: intraspecific social behavior. Both through its mother's behavior in various situations and through the experience of playing with her and its littermates, the puppy learns to interpret the various signals of body language and the language of sound and to adopt patterns of behavior. It is essential that the mother's behavior be normal. Nevertheless, despite the best upbringing, it sometimes happens that a puppy remains shy and mistrustful. In this case, the cause is likely to be an innate weakness of character.

Significance for the Dog Owner

In these first eight weeks of life, the breeder bears a great responsibility for the healthy development of the puppies. If they grow up in a spot remote from the breeder and his or her family, the environment, along with its important experiences, will remain a closed book for them. Serious behavioral problems may result. Moreover, the development of their brain will be stunted, which reduces their capacity for learning. Let the buyer beware, then. Choose the breeder carefully, and take a close look at the premises.

The Socialization Phase

The socialization phase, another of the imprinting phases, also marks the beginning of an important stage of life. It starts at roughly the beginning of the eighth week and ends, depending on the breed, between the twelfth and fourteenth weeks.

Puppies test their strength with other dogs the same age.

Living in a Community

The puppies of **undomesticated canines** gradually become acquainted with the entire pack during this phase. Older pack members are largely responsible for the majority of their remaining education. The young pups, or cubs, learn to become integrated into a group and to accept the rules that apply there. Equally important for the development of intraspecific social behavior is intensive play with littermates and other pack members. To an increasing extent, the pups also take the behaviors of the adult members of their species as models to be imitated.

With our **domestic dogs,** things are much the same. Just like its wild relatives, it is a social creature, directed toward a life within a defined group. That means that this stage of the puppy's life is characterized by three factors:
• a pronounced willingness to become integrated into a social unit,
• a great readiness to learn, and
• a strong play instinct.

Its interest in the world around it increases, and with it the puppy's need to explore that world. Its muscles and bones are exercised through play, and internal organs such as the heart and liver increase their functional capacity. The puppy learns to move with increasing sureness. As with its undomesticated kin, the foundations for smooth communication with other members of its species are laid at this time.

Moving into a New Home

During the socialization phase, the puppy usually goes to live with its new owner. In general, it is wise to bring the dog home at the beginning of this phase, so that you can make the best

Here the puppy needs a steady character and complete confidence in its human.

use of it. If the puppy is living at the breeder's under ideal conditions, with ample opportunity to explore its surroundings and play with its mother and siblings, you could possibly leave it there until the tenth week. In any event, the puppy should move to its new home before this important socialization phase ends.

In the following weeks, the groundwork is laid for a harmonious relationship between owner and pet. The separation from its mother and littermates, along with the move to unfamiliar surroundings, is a huge turning point in the puppy's life. For the time being, important developmental processes are interrupted. Instinctively the puppy feels lost without its pack. An abandoned wolf cub, for example, would inevitably perish in the wild. Now the puppy's instinct for self-preservation causes it to try to make friends with its new pack.

HOW-TO:
Puppy Behavior

Dogs communicate with one another and with humans by using body language, responding to changing facial expressions, barking, whimpering, and deciphering scent data. When you become familiar with these patterns of behavior, you will not only understand your puppy better, but also be able to deal with it more empathetically.

1 When they play, puppies practice social behavior among themselves.

Play Behavior
Drawings 1 and 4

When your puppy wants to play with you, it lowers the front of its body to the ground in front of you and may also bark at you. Alternatively, it may bring you one of its toys.

Young dogs that are highly self-assured frequently will take a sharp nip. If your puppy has this tendency, make it very

clear that such behavior is not allowed.

The Language of Sounds

The sounds it utters are the puppy's way of calling your attention either to itself or to something it has seen or heard. It is the dog's personality and its breed that determine whether it barks and whines frequently or rarely. The mother dog's behavior, too, has a role to play because the puppies adopt many of her ways. Whining and barking can mean a number of things:
• If it occurs frequently in new situations, it indicates a certain hypersensitivity and insecurity.
• At the door, it means that the little dog has to "go."
• Discomfort or pain are indicated if, for example, a puppy bites too hard when playing and the other dog lets out a howl and refuses to participate any more. In this way, young dogs learn to refrain from biting other members of their species.
• The puppy may bark happily when it greets you and when it invites you to play.

Submissive Behavior
Drawings 2 and 3

When dealing with higher-ranking dogs and human "top dogs," puppies make various gestures of submissiveness and appeasement. Trying to lick their humans' faces in greeting, for example, is nothing more than an energetic gesture of submission. Young and lower-ranking dogs that lick the muzzle of a higher-ranking dog are

2 A puppy greets higher-ranking dogs by licking their chops.

"requesting" a friendly welcome to the social unit. Offering a paw and making motions with a paw are also common occurrences. Such actions have their origin in the puppy's efforts to stimulate its mother's milk flow when nursing. This behavior is intended as a gesture of appeasement, and it is meant to be friendly and inviting. It may also be an invitation to play or a way of begging a human for something. Pushing its nose against you, which can mean that the puppy wants to be petted, is another of these behavioral patterns.

The supine (on-its-back-with-legs-up) position is a sign of passive submission. Again, this behavior has to do with social integration. At the same time, it is intended to inhibit the other dog's impulse to bite and to put that dog in a friendly mood. Puppies frequently display this behavior toward humans when greeting them. Particularly submissive puppies will urinate slightly at the same time. Don't scold your puppy; it wouldn't understand why it was being punished for submissiveness. Besides, this accompanying phenomenon will disappear of its own accord, apart from a few relapses, with increasing maturity.

The roots of this behavior also lie in earliest puppyhood. In the first three weeks of life, a puppy can urinate only when supine, with its mother massaging its belly with her tongue.

Threatening Behavior

Threatening behavior includes growling when the puppy is next to its food bowl and in similar situations. This is the little dog's way of seeing whether it can impress you—but don't let it succeed (see Further Integration, page 42)!

Sometimes you can observe elements of threatening behavior when puppies are playing together. If one gets too wild and stopping the game fails to improve things, the other puppy won't hesitate to bare its teeth to its playmate and growl menacingly. That usually has the desired effect, although it is not always long-lasting.

Body Language

To communicate through body language, the puppy uses its tail, ears, and coat. Its posture also contributes to the effect.

Tail: Wagging, with the puppy's tail raised high, is a sign of joyous excitement. Rapid wagging while the tail is lowered, with the puppy in a crouched position, indicates submissiveness. If the puppy is afraid, it also will go into a crouch and tuck its tail under.

Ears: If the young dog is alert and attentive, its ears are either pricked or pointed forward. Laid-back ears, depending on the situation, signify submissiveness or insecurity. Alternatively, they may be a part of the threatening behavior pattern (warding off).

Coat: When the hair on its back stands on end, the puppy is trying to look bigger, in order to impress another puppy. It also bristles when it has seen something that makes it feel uneasy.

Unfortunately, as a result of breed-specific characteristics, it is no longer possible for all dogs to use their body language correctly. It may be that a dog's tail has been docked, its ears can no longer be pricked, or its coat is too long. To prevent communication problems among dogs, it is essential to put your puppy in contact with other dogs its own age (see Imprinting and Play Days for Puppies, page 58).

3 Lying on its back is a gesture of submissiveness.

The Exhausted Puppy

Puppies need a great deal of sleep, and often they fall asleep quite suddenly. It happens repeatedly that a young dog all at once will lie down during a game and be sound asleep. Don't wake your pet. If you're out for a walk and notice that your little dog is lagging behind or even sits down, don't encourage it to continue the walk. These are signs of fatigue. If possible just carry it home.

4 Playing together is fun, and it also teaches the puppy important rules of living together.

With the mother dog nearby, the surroundings can be explored without anxiety.

Significance for the Dog Owner

For all intents and purposes, this phase is the time in which the foundations for a lifelong bond of human and canine closeness are laid. Such a relationship can be created by devoting plenty of time to your puppy and keeping it close to you as much as possible. Take the little dog seriously; that is, think of the puppy during this crucial stage as a real dog, not as a cuddly toy.

From the very outset, you need to follow the same rules that will apply later on, when the puppy is grown. A dog can't understand why it was allowed in your bed as a puppy but now, as a full-grown dog, suddenly has to sleep in its crate. It doesn't realize that it used to be sweet and tiny, but now weighs some 88 pounds (40 kg) and is 28 inches (70 cm) tall at the shoulders. A dog needs exact rules that it can follow now and rely on to remain valid later, if it is to develop trust, a sense of security, and an ability to adapt to new situations. If such rules are in place, it will accept its human social partners and feel safe and secure in its "family."

Playing Together Is Important

In the socialization phase, playing with you is of great importance for the puppy. Not only does it enjoy this appropriate kind of attention, but the activity also contributes substantially to the formation of a close bond. If you occasionally issue the invitation to play yourself or decide when the game is over, you will simultaneously let the puppy know that you are the "pack leader." By playing, puppies also learn to inhibit their impulse to bite humans. Don't allow your pet to snap at parts of your body or your clothing (see Training a Puppy, Step-by-Step pages 46–59). When the little dog is tired after playing, you could lie down beside it on the rug and imitate canine contact behavior. This, too, will promote a close bond and give the dog confidence.

Many Experiences of Its Environment

In this stage of life, you need to schedule joint activities, as well as your puppy's first training sessions. During your outing, gradually offer your pet a multitude of experiences of the environment; that will help it develop in a positive way. Avoid inundating it with experiences, however.

In my opinion, a dog can't be friendly enough in this day and age. Give your puppy plenty of contact with humans, even if it is slated to become a watchdog later on. If it possesses a certain breed-related guard instinct, it will certainly not lose that through contact with people. On the other hand, a dog that lacks social contacts can become overly mistrustful, misinterpret inherently nonthreatening situations, and react in the wrong way.

Because the socialization phase is, as stated earlier, an imprinting phase, the puppy should become acquainted with everything that will be part of its life in the future. Take the puppy for a walk in town now and then. Show it all possible types of terrain—meadows, asphalt surfaces, gravel, and the like. Let it walk on a variety of flooring types, including tiles, wood, and carpeting, or go up and down stairs occasionally, to prevent danger later on (see HOW-TO: Eliminating Hazards, page 18). On walks you can incorporate little "adventures," for example, by leading the puppy across a fallen tree trunk or climbing over a bank of earth. All these things promote a feeling of belonging together.

The socialization phase is the time of life when a puppy acquires crucial behavioral patterns by watching adult members of its species. Puppies need ample contact with dogs of normal disposition and of all ages, especially those of their own age.

Note: If your puppy seems somewhat unsure in a normal situation, pass over this behavior and make light of it. You will only reinforce the dog's fearfulness by petting it or picking it up and making a big deal out of the incident.

Behavior with Other Members of Its Species

Practicing social behavior among others of its kind, which also occurs in this phase, is rudely interrupted by the puppy's separation from its mother and siblings. The continuation of this development is up to you. Give the puppy a chance to meet dogs of all ages with a good disposition. If you're in doubt about a specific dog's disposition, ask the owner whether his dog is tolerant of puppies. Playing with other dogs of the same age is also quite important, but it is sometimes difficult to find other puppies.

My tip: To find playmates, you might seek out dog training classes where other puppy owners may come. Ask breed clubs and similar organizations about puppy play days or imprinting play days. They are well worth attending (see page 58). Some puppy owners tend to protect their dogs from everything and to pick them up at once when they sight other four-legged creatures. All you will do is eventually make your dog either fearful and distraught or aggressive with other members of its species.

Further Integration

In the months that follow, your puppy gradually will outgrow its baby shoes. Until it is completely grown, however, its development will continue in some areas. Let us next take another look at the life of our domesticated dog's wild ancestors, the wolves.

I f you can't teach your young dog in the integration phase that you are a good pack leader, there will never be a strong bond of trust between you and your pet.

The Development of Hierarchy

In the socialization phase, the wolf cubs developed strong bonds to one another and to their pack. Now a hierarchy, or order of rank, begins to develop.

In the community of the litter: The development of hierarchy begins within the community of the litter in the following weeks, roughly during the fourth month of life. In playful confrontations, each cub tries to find out where the others' strengths and weaknesses lie. Physical superiority tends to be relegated to the background. The wild games of racing and pursuit at this age are an important way of intensively training the cubs' bodies for the first wider-ranging excursions with the entire pack.

In the pack: In addition, the cubs are increasingly developing a better understanding and acceptance of authority. Instinctively they know that a pack is able to survive only if headed by a capable lead animal. They willingly subordinate themselves to such a pack leader and enjoy the security and trust he conveys to them through his intelligent, superior manner. By the time the young wolves are about one year old, each will have found its place in the pack. In addition, a strong feeling of belonging together will have developed. This is important both for a harmonious life together and for effective cooperation on their joint hunting expeditions.

Physically the young wolves are now able to run even lengthy distances without overtiring themselves. Now they are allowed to accompany the adults on their first hunting expeditions, though without actually participating in them. They are told to lie down, so to speak, and allowed to watch everything from a certain distance, so that they can imitate the grown-ups one day.

Significance for the Dog Owner

With domesticated dogs, too, this phase begins during the fourth month, approximately; it may be somewhat delayed, however, depending on the breed. This means that during the following days and weeks, you will see what kind of bonding has occurred and what your dog's relationship with you is. The irretrievable imprinting phases are now largely over, and everything experienced thus far, aside from hereditary factors, will have a substantial influence on the dog's further development. If your puppy was still with its littermates, a hierarchy would develop within the litter, as it does among wolf cubs. Because the puppy by this time is already in its new family's home, one hopes, its human partners have to substitute for its littermates, so to speak. The puppy now will use them to test how far it can go or how capable the "pack leader" is.

For example, the young dog may start to defend its food dish or other objects, such as bones or toys, by growling. Alternatively, it may try to call into question certain rules that it has observed faithfully until now. It may steal something from the dinner table or the kitchen counter or disregard your instructions during your daily training sessions. Some young dogs can become rather wild and disrespectful, so that games with their humans occasionally get out of hand.

A dog should not be walked without a leash.

Being Consistent

The extent to which this change in your dog is noticeable depends both on its personality and on the course of the preceding imprinting phases. If your four-legged friend is very willing to subordinate itself and if its development thus far has been excellent, you will notice little. With a so-called "alpha dog," on the other hand, particularly one that may have had little training, this phase can be all the more pronounced.

It is now up to you and the other members of your family to show the dog not only that you aren't going to relinquish your "alpha" position, but also that you are thoroughly capable of leading the "pack." Consistency is one of the most important things in the training of dogs, and it is especially essential during this phase.

Insist that the current rules be observed, and don't give in to your rowdy teenager when it tries to "test" you. As with young wolves, your strategic qualities are what really matter, not the demonstration of physical superiority. If your young dog defends

Playing with your puppy cultivates close bonding.

a bone, for example, don't hit it. Take the bone away from it firmly, and don't give it back until the little rascal behaves in a friendly way again. The daily obedience exercises will give the young dog additional help in becoming part of a social unit.

Continue to work on developing the relationship between you and your pet. For example, you can hide during one of your walks, without saying a word. Don't go too far away, of course. When, after a certain length of time, the little dog starts searching for you, you can say a few words to help it along in case it doesn't find you right away. Show that you're overjoyed when it finally locates you.

My tip: If your dog displays undesirable behavior in a situation, you should deliberately recreate this situation over and over again. If it growls when at its food dish, it would be wrong to take that as a reason to let it eat undisturbed from now on. Instead, keep taking the dish away from it until the growling stops.

If you are inconsistent or the various members of your family treat the dog differently, it can't determine its exact place in the pack and won't know who is "top dog." Then it will become insecure. Depending on your pet's personality, it may develop a variety of problems, including behavioral disturbances. A highly self-confident young dog will more or less train itself and, once grown, establish order in the pack and assume the role of leader. This can become very unpleasant.

It is a different matter if you have treated your puppy properly during the first six months. You will know you have done so if you have become the center of your pet's life. Its bond to you will be very strong, and on

The young dog should obey the Come command immediately.

your joint outings it will—despite a pronounced desire to explore—always strive not to lose sight of you.

Looking Ahead

Although this book is concerned primarily with the first six months of your dog's life, we would like to take a brief look at the second six months. This is the time when the dog reaches puberty.

During this stage, some dogs now and then fail to react correctly to visual and sound signals. If that happens, try to neutralize the situation in a playful way and to distract your pet, just as you did in puppyhood. Some young dogs become less obedient, ignore quite a few commands, and often expand their radius of action too greatly. Keep on training it consistently and constantly, and don't let your four-legged friend experience any undesirable success. For example, your dog may no longer obey when it sees other members of its species. Either put on its leash in good time, or attach a piece of clothesline about 66 feet (20 m) long to its collar, so that the dog drags it along the ground. Then, when your pet ignores your call, the line will serve as a kind of emergency brake. In addition, try to distract your dog (see Chasing, page 58).

Training a Puppy, Step-by-Step

Training a Dog Is Important

Every dog, whether big or small, should be given careful training. That is the prerequisite for a problem-free life for both pet and owner. However, only a very few people are aware that the training process must begin in puppyhood. Obedience, good conduct, and reliable behavior in our civilized world will be displayed unhesitatingly by your pet only if these things have been imprinted early in its life.

Unfortunately, even today some people still cling to very old-fashioned notions of training. For example, they think a puppy doesn't comprehend anything anyway, so there is no reason to start training until it is a year old. Or they say a young dog must be leashed as much as possible, and similar things. We now know which elementary processes are under way during the first few months of a puppy's development. You can easily imagine what improper care or a lack of appropriate stimuli in these phases can cause in a young dog.

When that same dog is suddenly asked to learn obedience at the age of one, it means a decisive turning point in its life. Apart from the fact that the training will be very costly in most cases, the dog very rarely will obey as reliably as an animal taught these lessons in puppyhood. When you bring a little puppy into your home, therefore, you need to be aware that although appropriate attention and training require an enormous amount of time and commitment, it is all in the best interest of the dog.

Taking Advantage of the Puppy's Willingness to Learn

As mentioned previously, a puppy is very willing to learn and also has a pronounced desire to play. In addition, it shows great interest in communicating with its humans, as if it knew that its survival depends on them. These are ideal conditions for imparting the basic rules of living together to the little dog. The prerequisite is that you view the puppy from the outset as a real dog and not try to endow it with human attributes.

Consistency is the first requirement in all areas of training. If you take that to heart, your puppy will effortlessly learn that carpet fringes, chair legs, and the like are taboo and will happily master its first lessons. The emphasis here is on happily. The point of all the training is not slavish obedience; instead, owner and pet should form a team in which the dog trustingly acknowledges its partner and obeys gladly, not out of fear or some similar motivation. This is the only way to end up with a full-grown dog that truly enriches your family life. You need not fear that the dog will make a negative impression, fail to return when it is off leash, or something of the kind.

Establishing a Bond

A close, trusting bond between you and your four-legged housemate is another prerequisite for successful training. This bond does not develop automatically; you must actively work on it!

Raising: Keep the puppy near you as much as possible. You should never just leave it in the backyard. Keeping a dog by itself and away from you runs contrary to the needs of the species. Even though full-grown dogs need to stay in the backyard sometimes, they still need as much close contact with you as possible.

Sleeping spot: In choosing the spot where you want the dog to sleep, keep in mind the little dog's needs. It goes against the puppy's nature to spend the night alone. That doesn't mean that it has to sleep in your bedroom or in your bed. Putting its crate fairly near your bedroom is sufficient. The puppy should always have the feeling that you are nearby. Let the puppy know that sleeping time is for sleeping, not for whining and crying.

Walking: On daily walks in suitable areas, let your little puppy off leash in fenced and safe areas only after an adjustment period of several days. That will prompt the pup to keep an eye on your whereabouts on its own. Simultaneously, it will let the puppy follow its desire to explore. If you want it to come to you, call its name clearly. If it fails to obey at once, walk a short distance away in the opposite direction or hide behind a bush. When

the pup thinks it has been left behind alone, the little dog's instinct will tell it that it is in danger. Consequently, it will try with all its might to find you as soon as possible. A highly self-confident dog will take longer to search than a more cautious one. If you behave this way consistently from the outset, your dog will always maintain contact with you later on, because that was what it experienced in the imprinting phases.

If your little dog ever gets so involved in something that you doubt whether it really will come, it is best to simply go and get it, without much calling and carrying on. Never run after your pet; it would interpret that as an invitation to race. If you just stand and wait, too, there is no reason why it should come. After all, it can see and hear you. Never call a puppy to you for punishment. This will teach it not to come to you.

The puppy learns the Down command, too, through positive conditioning. Offering it a dog biscuit and stroking its back induce the puppy to lie down.

The daily walks should last no more than 10 minutes at the start, to keep from overworking the young dog. Take several short walks a day, rather than one long walk The puppy needs to move, not to be moved. The older it is, the longer the walks can become.

Lessons: The little daily obedience lessons also strengthen the bond, as do companion dog training and, later on, special training courses. A dog forms the closest bond with the person who offers it appropriate activity, not the one who pampers and feeds it.

The Right Motivation

As previously stated, you should not try to engage your dog in a kind of robotlike parade-ground drill. Your goal, rather, is to teach it to obey cheerfully. Practice with your puppy without exerting pressure, and make the "work" so pleasant that it participates gladly and voluntarily. This is called positive conditioning.

"I won't play any more if you bite too hard." In this way, young dogs learn to refrain from biting other members of their species.

• Praise and encouragement, as well as little treats as a reward, play an important role. Show how overjoyed you are when your puppy rushes cheerfully to you when called. When doing leash training, for example, talk to your four-legged companion in a friendly way and entice it by making encouraging noises, such as clicking your tongue. Then it will participate enthusiastically. If you trot listlessly beside your dog, it will jog along just as lethargically, or perhaps even start to tug at the leash.

• Your mental attitude, too, has an influence on the training process. If you are disinterested or uncertain, that attitude will be transferred to your puppy. If you approach the young dog decisively, however, it can sense more of what you want of it and can react to your commands more quickly.

• Don't overdo it with the young dog if you want it to keep enjoying the joint training sessions. Three 5-minute sessions a day are sufficient. Gradually increase the sessions to about half an hour per day, spread over the course of the day, by the time the puppy is six months old. Always practice new exercises at home first, without any distractions, and include some distracting elements only as the dog increases in ability and age.

• Variety will also make the training more fun. Never ask your puppy to repeat the same exercise it knows very well many times in succession. If a lesson has been well learned, leave things at that and go on to another. On the other hand, if a command was not carried out very well, repeat it and give the dog a little support. Make it a rule to start and end every "instruction period" with an exercise that the little dog already knows. This allows the puppy to end on a success and with the praise it knows you will give it for that success.

Praise and Reprimands and a "Guilty Conscience"

Sometimes a dog is praised or reprimanded at the wrong time, so that you accomplish precisely the opposite of what you want to accomplish. That happens when you measure the animal's feelings with a human yardstick. A dog has no sense of good and evil in our meaning of those terms nor does it have a guilty conscience. Rather, it guides its behavior primarily according to what outcome is pleasant or unpleasant.

It is important always to praise or reprimand immediately, in a way that the dog can clearly understand (see HOW-TO: Training, pages 50–51).

Gripping and shaking the back of the puppy's neck is an appropriate form of censure.

HOW-TO: Training

Careful training is the basis upon which owner and pet can live together in harmony. Consequently, it is important to observe certain ground rules from the start. Only then can your puppy learn what you want of it and become the pleasant, obedient companion you desire, a pet that can safely go with you almost anywhere.

1 The puppy's place is next to the armchair.

Unity Within the Family

It is important to impart a sense of security and trust to the little dog and to make clear just where it fits in the pack. All the members of the family, therefore, must pull together. If a certain room is supposed to be off limits to the dog, for example, no one can secretly give the puppy access to it. Each family member must

know the rules and, for the sake of the puppy, live by them.

Being Consistent
Drawing 1

All the rules that will apply to the grown dog later must be in force for the puppy right now, at all times. If you're reading the newspaper in your armchair and don't want a 110-pound (50-kg) Saint Bernard on your lap, you should forbid such behavior for a 30-pound (14-kg) Saint Bernard puppy. The adult dog will reasonably expect to go everywhere the puppy was allowed to go.

Communicating with the Dog
Drawing 2

Dogs usually react quite well to the human voice and to human body language. Therefore you should use a variety of different registers with your pet. Give commands in a firm, but not loud, voice. For praise, use a high, cheerful voice. The dog's joy at your praise should be plain to see. Try several pitches to see which one gets the best reaction from your puppy. Reprimand it in a stern voice, somewhat louder if necessary.

Your body language, too, will convey important information to your dog. Your puppy will not come to you, for example, if you approach it at your full height, with a threatening look and the words "Now you come here." If you bend over and back away, however, beckoning it to follow, it will rush to you happily.

2 Moving away prompts the puppy to come after you.

Only One Person Does the Training

Even a puppy can begin to learn some obedience exercises. To help your pet understand the commands, appoint one adult in your family to practice with the dog during the first few weeks. Otherwise, it is too difficult for it to learn the individual commands and to get used to different voices at the same time. Bit by bit, the other family members can practice with the puppy too, but they all should use the same commands.

Give Clear Commands

Keep the commands brief and clear, so that the puppy can hear the individual words. Call its name to get its attention; then give the command.

Have Commands Obeyed at Once

The dog should obey your command no later than the second time it is given. If your puppy has understood the meaning of a command but doesn't obey the first time, support it with a little corrective measure. As long as the puppy sits on command, for example, say nothing, but if it gets up, repeat the command. If you keep on talking to the dog, even though it is performing the exercise correctly, its attention will eventually wander.

Always Release

After the dog has carried out a command, you must terminate it, either by going on to another exercise or by ending the training time. For example; if you've given the down command to make your puppy lie down, don't just leave it there. Tell it to sit again after a short time. If the dog is not released from the command, it will never learn how long it must perform an exercise. That will make it unsure, and it will never obey reliably.

3 Gripping the puppy's jaws is an appropriate form of reprimand.

Have Exercises Performed Exactly

Not only does each of the obedience exercises follow a certain course, but each one also differs from all the others. To help your young dog adjust to them and know exactly what is being asked of it, it is important that you always have it perform the exercises correctly. This persistence will give the dog the security it needs and reinforce its trust in you. It won't understand why it is allowed to do an exercise sloppily one day and then is punished for mistakes the next.

Praise and Reprimand
Drawings 3 and 4

Through praise and reprimand, a dog learns to repeat cheerfully everything connected with pleasant sensations and to avoid behavior connected with unpleasant ones.

Praise: To let the puppy know that it has done something correctly, praise it lavishly immediately after its good behavior by using a pleasant tone of voice, stroking it, and/or offering a few little treats. The dog has to plainly show its happiness at receiving praise.

Watch to see how your puppy expresses its joy (see Communicating with the Dog, page 50).

Reprimand: If, on the other hand, your pet does something you don't like, you should reprimand it immediately after it has "goofed." The punishment must be something appropriate

4 Praise is reinforced with a little treat.

for a dog, something it can understand. Suitable punishments include, for example, a loudly uttered "No," in conjunction with the appropriate body language, or a pointed ending of the session. Also suitable is putting your hand over the puppy's muzzle, exerting a slight pressure on its chops, if necessary. Alternatively, you might shake the skin on its nape or, if the puppy has a very thick coat, hold it firmly in the supine position.

Try these methods to see which gets the best reaction from your puppy. There are dogs on whom a loud "No" makes a sufficient impression. Others, however, react only when you shake the back of their neck vigorously.

For the Heel the puppy walks on the left.

The puppy learns the Sit.

Confusing praise and reprimand: We commonly make the mistake of punishing the dog, for example, when it comes only after being called repeatedly. That links the punishment not with the delayed return but rather with the very act of returning. Instead of motivating the dog to come more quickly in the future, it achieves exactly the opposite.

A puppy that has this experience learns a lifelong lesson—that nothing good awaits it when it obeys a human's summons. Its "bad conscience" is nothing but a subservient, insecure behavior motivated by fear of the punishment administered for reasons the dog does not comprehend. The fact that it comes nevertheless speaks in its favor. Always praise your pet when it obeys—even if it seems to take forever and you're about to burst with impatience.

Unconsciously rewarding your pet for misbehavior causes similar problems. For example, when your doorbell rings and your dog barks incessantly, you want your dog to stop. However, all you do is pet it and say in a friendly voice that everything is all right. As a result, the dog interprets your behavior as a reinforcement of its own actions and continues to bark vigorously.

What Your Puppy Must Learn

A description of the individual exercises that your dog should master while still a puppy follow. You can teach it certain commands both in spoken form and as hand signals. With either type, you also can use a whistled signal; it is very easily remembered and often more successful than a spoken command. It adds more variety to the training process; additionally, your puppy will learn to react to different "languages." At the beginning of each exercise, we tell you how the command sounds or what the hand signal looks like. The whistled signal is included as a special tip.

Responding to Its Name

The first lesson your puppy needs to master is to respond to its name. Always call your pet in connection with something pleasant—feeding or petting, for example—so that the little dog will quickly learn to react positively.

It may be a good idea to talk to the breeder and select a name for the puppy ahead of time; then the puppy can get used to it before joining your household. That will make the adjustment to a new home a little easier.

The Sit

The Sit is one of the easiest exercises, and most puppies learn it very quickly.
• Command: "Sit."
• Hand signal: Raised hand or raised right index finger.

How to practice: Put the puppy on leash, and take the leash in your left hand (see Getting Used to the Collar and Leash, page 17). With your right hand, hold a little treat slightly above the dog's head and give the command, combined with the dog's name.

Repeat it from time to time and wait for your four-legged friend to sit down. It will do so sooner or later, in order to look up at the treat more

comfortably. When it is seated, wait just a moment, then give your pet the treat and praise it. Scratching its chest will help keep it in a seated position. As the puppy's ability increases, cut back on the treats.

After your young dog understands the command, it should sit the first time. If not, place your right hand on its collar, gently pressing its hindquarters downward with your left. As you do so, say "Sit" again. Don't forget to praise your pet when it obeys. Always have the dog sit before its leash is put on or removed and before it eats, and don't forget to release it from the command (see HOW-TO: Training, pages 50–51).

The **hand signal** can be taught along with the oral command. Every time you say "Sit," show the puppy your raised hand or raised index finger. Soon it will sit in response to the hand signal alone.

With a little help the puppy goes into the Down.

The Down

The Down drill is very important because later on you also can use it to direct your pet to lie down somewhere by itself. It has to be relied on to stay there until you come for it. Your puppy, of course, is too young to be left alone (see Staying Alone, page 56). Start this exercise as soon as the puppy has learned the Sit.
• Command: "Down."
• Hand signal: Downward movement with your right hand.

How to practice: For this exercise, too, put your dog on leash and have it sit at your left side. Crouch down next to it and, using your left hand, hold the leash on the ground in front of the dog, allowing no slack in the leash. Next, with a little treat in your right hand, move your hand in a downward arc from the dog's nose to the ground, then along the ground, a little in front of your pet. At the same time, give the command "Down" along with the puppy's name.

Hand signal: The puppy will learn the accompanying downward hand movement automatically, so to speak.

To get the reward, the puppy will soon lie down. While it eats the treat, stroke its back to encourage the puppy to maintain the position. As you do so, say "Down" again. After a short time, have the puppy sit again. Then you can let it stand up. If possible, conclude the exercise before the puppy stands up of its own accord. Here, too, gradually decrease the treats. Should the young dog refuse to obey after it has mastered the exercise, correct it by gently pushing its withers down to the ground. Don't forget the praise!

My tip: As soon as the puppy understands the verbal command, add the whistled signal. It is a long-drawn-out whistle on the broad side of the training whistle used with hunting dogs. In this way you can train the dog to lie down on its own when it hears the whistle. Later, your pet will learn to do that some distance away from you, which can be extremely useful in some situations.

Leash Training

Some puppies accept the leash without any problems from the very outset; others do not (see Getting Used to the Collar and Leash, page 17). If your pet belongs to the latter group, it is best to let the dog lead you at first; that is, you should go wherever it wants. After a short time, it will become used to the leash, and you can start the exercise.

If the puppy is destined to be trained as a hunting dog, it must learn to retrieve early.

- Command: "Heel."

How to practice: For the position, the dog walks at your left. In that way, when your dog is fully trained, your right hand will be free. "Heel" can't mean sometimes at your left and sometimes at your right.

Begin with the basic position, with the puppy sitting at your left. Take the leash in your right hand, letting it hang loosely, but without being too long. In your left hand, hold the time-tested treat. Now give the command and start walking at a fairly lively pace. The dog's head should be about even with your knee as it follows along, staying close to your side and with the leash hanging loosely. Keep talking encouragingly to your pet (see The Right Motivation, page 48). If your pupil can smell the treat, that will be enough. When you stop, have the dog sit and give it its reward.

If the puppy tries to drag you forward or to one side, don't pull it back. Instead, try to motivate it by making yourself more interesting (see page 48). Try getting the little dog more interested in you by using different treats, such as small pieces of sausage or a toy.

When you are ready to end the Heel and let the dog off leash again, have it sit while you remove the leash. Then wait a moment before saying "Go." The dog should not connect being let off leash with dashing off immediately.

At first, walk short distances, always going straight ahead. Incorporate curves and sharp turns gradually, once everything is working well. As with all the other exercises, you should gradually cut back on the treats.

My tip: If you hold the treat in such a way that the dog neither forges ahead nor lags behind, it will automatically learn to stay in the correct position.

Coming When Called

Coming when called, one of the most important exercises, is also the exercise dog owners are most concerned about. It should be designed so that the dog never has an opportunity "not to hear" the command. In contrast to the other exercises, you will have a hard time correcting the puppy when it is far away and fails to come when called.

- Command: "Come."

How to practice: Start the exercise in connection with the puppy's mealtimes. While you're preparing the food in the kitchen, another family member should keep the puppy in another room or in the yard. Then call its name and give the Come command. It will race happily and quickly to you to get its food. If you consistently proceed in this manner during the imprinting phases, the little dog will note that it has no other choice than to come to you when you say "Come."

At first, never use the command during a walk. Only when it is working smoothly at home and has stuck in the little dog's mind can you try it outdoors. Proceed as outlined in Establishing a Bond (see page 47). Only when the puppy is already running straight toward you anyway and is only a few yards away should you say "Come." Very gradually, start to use "Come" to call the dog from slightly greater distances. As soon as it comes, shower it with praise and give it a treat.

My tip: As soon as your puppy understands "Come," you can use the whistled signal in combination with the verbal command, even while the imprinting phases are still under way. Using the narrow side of the whistle used for training hunting dogs, blow two so-called double whistles in rapid succession. Soon the puppy will react to the whistle alone.

Letting Go of Something

In another exercise, the puppy must relinquish whatever it has to you on command.

• Command: "Let go."

How to practice: If your dog has something in its mouth that it shouldn't, just go up to it and take it away, using the command "Let go." If it won't relinquish the object, press one hand gently against its flews until the puppy opens its mouth. Then praise it and give it a treat or some other object it is allowed to have. It is very important to remain calm; otherwise, you will transfer your agitation to the dog, and it may try to escape with its booty.

The Stay

This exercise prepares the dog to maintain the down position at a certain spot later on, even in your absence.

• Commands: "Sit" and "Stay."

How to practice: Start this exercise after your dog has learned the Sit. Put it on leash and say "Sit; Stay." Then step out a little distance in front of the puppy. After a short time, before it gets restless again, go back to it and praise it. Very gradually, increase your distance from the dog until you are at most one full leash-length away. Make sure to keep the leash slack; otherwise, the dog will stand up. If your pet stays seated calmly while you face it, you can begin slowly walking back and forth, still staying in front of it. Keep fairly close at first, then increase the distance gradually. The dog should stay on leash. The Down–Stay is practiced the same way, but with the dog lying down.

Note: Correct the dog immediately if it leaves the designated place, even if it is a matter of only a few inches.

If you want to have your puppy specially trained later, it needs to become acquainted with typical surroundings during the imprinting phases.

Staying Alone

Naturally, dogs are eager to be taken along everywhere you go. There are times when that is impossible, however. For this reason, every canine needs to learn to stay home alone for a few hours. If properly trained, that presents no problem. However, don't start the training until the young dog is about four or five months old. Being left alone too early can trigger severe fear of abandonment in a puppy, because it instinctively knows that it is lost (see The Developmental Phases of Puppies, page 31). Even if it doesn't howl, that is no indication that it feels no anxiety. Some puppies go into a kind of apathetic state when they feel abandoned. It is especially serious for puppies left alone if, for example, a low-flying aircraft thunders over the house or something else happens that frightens them. Such negative experiences in the imprinting phase can make the dog unable to stay alone without problems ever again.

How to practice: It's best to start getting the puppy accustomed to being alone when it is tired—after playing, for example. Put down something for it to nibble on, a rawhide roll or the like, to keep it busy in case it becomes active. Next, leave your home for a few minutes, to go to the mailbox, for example. If you hear the dog howling, go back and reprimand it, saying "No." Then leave it again. If the puppy stays quiet, praise it when you go back in. Very gradually, lengthen the periods of time when the dog stays alone.

Riding in a Car

Most dogs enjoy riding in a car. Some, however, don't take to this activity immediately. Consequently, you need to get your puppy used to

During puppy play days, young dogs become acquainted with a great many new things.

car trips when it is young. Dogs are always safest when put in a carrier for all car trips. Some people use seat belts for their pets, but carriers are still best.

How to practice: At first, take the puppy along only on short trips. In the beginning, always have a second person present to look after the pup during the trip. The puppy should eat nothing during the hours before you leave home. Immediately after the trip, however, there should always be something nice awaiting it, such as a time of playing or a special treat. In that way, you can make the experience of riding in a car more enjoyable for your puppy.

If your puppy has problems with car sickness, ask your veterinarian to recommend a suitable medication.

Preventing Undesirable Behaviors

Over the course of time, some dogs acquire annoying habits, such as begging, jumping up on people, or chasing cars, joggers, and other moving objects. The origins of such bad behaviors are usually discernible even in puppyhood or adolescence. You need to take appropriate preventive measures here.

Begging at the table: You can prevent begging at the table by simply refusing to feed the puppy at the table from the very outset. Remain firm, even if your pet gives you heart-rending looks; if need be, lock it out of the room for the remainder of the meal. Some owners think their dog will be content if it just gets something once, but the opposite is the case. That will be only the start of its begging.

Jumping up on people: To discourage the puppy's habit of jumping up or to keep it from developing the habit in the first place, always bend over when you greet your pet. Respond to jumping up with a clear "No." Greet the little dog in a friendly way and at some length, to show it that you will enter into contact with it even if it doesn't jump up. It is important that all the people who greet the puppy behave in the same fashion.

Chasing: Make it clear to your puppy or young dog early on that you don't want such behavior. Even if it looks cute when the little butterball pursues someone on a bike yet fails to catch him. If the puppy tries to take off while leashed, show it—with a sharp tug on the leash and a "No"— what you expect of it. If it is off leash, try your best to grab it while it is preparing for its "take-off." Alternatively, try to distract the young dog with a treat or its favorite toy.

Imprinting and Play Days

Attending "puppy kindergarten" is highly recommended. At these encounters, during the socialization phase puppies learn intraspecific social behavior while playing with other puppies of approximately the same age. This is important for smooth association with other members of the species later on. In addition, the puppies are introduced to a variety of visual and acoustic stimuli. Moreover, the owner learns how to deal with his or her little four-legged creature correctly and has a chance to practice some initial obedience tasks.

Early Encouragement of Puppies to Be Trained as Utility Dogs

Dogs that are scheduled to undergo special training later on, for example, as hunting dogs or rescue dogs, should become acquainted with their future surrounding field while still in the imprinting phases.
• A future hunting dog, ideally, should be introduced to feathers and skins while in puppyhood. Praise it whenever it brings you something, even a half-decayed mouse. That will encourage it to retrieve, because such activity is always great fun for the little dog.
• A puppy that is slated for use in rescue work should be taken regularly to a rescue dog training ground. There it can become acquainted with the special training devices and situations and watch "colleagues" at work.
• Agility and other types of sports involving skill can be introduced to the little dog early. Have it crawl through a little flexible tunnel or, with your help, try a few steps on the crosswalk. The puppy is not yet ready for jumping, however.

• Greyhound puppies that are destined for racing should likewise get to know the racetrack, the artificial hare, and the starting box during puppyhood.

It is important that the puppy, in all these early contacts with its subsequent field of duties, have good experiences exclusively and not become overly tired. The special training courses themselves don't start until the dog is about one year old and physically able to handle the demands. **My tip:** If you already own a well-trained dog and want to bring a puppy into your household and give it the same training, you will have a relatively easy time. The young dog will model itself closely on its adult cohort and adopt many of its behaviors.

The little puppy is already able to crawl through a fabric tunnel. Early training in such skills is good preparation for participation in agility training later on.

Index

Addresses and Suggested Readings

Canine Organizations
The American Kennel Club
5580 Centerview Drive
Suite 200
Raleigh, NC 27606-3390

The addresses of dog clubs
and organizations are available
from the AKC.

Liability Insurance
Some insurance companies
now offer liability insurance
policies for dogs.

Books
American Kennel Club, *The
Complete Dog Book* (Howell
Book House, Inc., New
House, Inc., New York,
1992).

Alderton, David, *The Dog Care
Manual* (Barron's Educational
Series, Inc., Hauppauge, New
York, 1986).

Bailey, Gwen, *The Well
Behaved Dog* (Barron's
Educational Series, Inc.,
Hauppauge, New York,
1998).

Baer, Ted, *Communicating
With Your Dog* (Barron's
Educational Series, Inc.,
Hauppauge, New York,
1989).

Baer, Ted, *How To Teach Your
Old Dog New Tricks*
(Barron's Educational Series,
Inc., Hauppauge, New York,
1991).

Coile, D. Caroline, *Show Me!*
(Barron's Educational Series,
Inc., Hauppauge, New York,
1997).

Klever, Ulrich, *The Complete
Book of Dog Care* (Barron's
Educational Series, Inc.,
Hauppauge, New York,
1995).

Pinney, Chris C., DVM,
*Caring for Your Older
Pet* (Barron's Educational
Series, Inc., Hauppauge,
New York, 1995).

Pinney Chris C., DVM,
*Guide to Home Pet
Grooming* (Barron's
Educational Series, Inc.,
Hauppauge, New York,
1991).

Schlegl-Kofler, Katharina,
Educating Your Dog (Barron's
Educational Series, Inc.,
Hauppauge, New York,
1996).

Smith, Cheryl S., *Pudgy Pooch,
Picky Pooch* (Barron's
Educational Series, Inc.,
Hauppauge, New York,
1998).

Taunton, Stephanie J., and
Cheryl S. Smith, *The Trick is
in the Training* (Barron's
Educational Series, Inc.,
Hauppauge, New York,
1998).

Wegler, Monika, *Dogs: A
Complete Pet Owner's
Manual* (Barron's Educational
Series, Inc., Hauppauge, New
York, 1992).

Wrede, Barbara J., *Before You
Buy That Puppy* (Barron's
Educational Series, Inc.,
Hauppauge, New York,
1994).

Wrede, Barbara J., *Civilizing
Your Puppy* (Barron's
Educational Series, Inc.,
Hauppauge, New York,
1989).

Magazines
Dog World
29 Wacker Drive
Chicago, IL 60606-3298
(312) 726-2802

Dog Fancy
P. O. Box 53264
Boulder, CO 80322-3264
(303) 666-8504

A ball for the dog to chase should be made of solid rubber.

Important Note

This guide tells the reader how to buy, care for, and train puppies. The author and the publisher consider it important to point out that the rules given in this guide are meant primarily for normally developed young dogs from a good breeder—that is, healthy dogs of good character. If the puppy comes from an animal shelter, it may be possible to get some information on the dog's origin and peculiarities there. Certain breeds are not suitable for first-time dog owners; they belong in the hands of people who have experience with dogs (see page 7).

Even well-trained and carefully supervised puppies sometimes do damage to someone else's property or even cause accidents. It is in the owner's interest to be adequately insured against such eventualities: We strongly urge all dog owners to purchase a liability policy that covers their dog.

About the Author

Katharina Schlegl-Kofler has been involved with the appropriate keeping and training of dogs for many years. She owns retrievers. For years, she has conducted play days for puppies and training courses for dogs of all breeds.

About the Photographer

Christine Steimer has been a freelance photographer since 1985. In 1989 she decided to specialize in animal photography, and since that time she has done work for several magazines. The photograph on the inside back cover was taken by Monika Wegler.

About the Illustrator

György Jankovics studied at the academies of art in Budapest and Hamburg. He draws animal and plant subjects for a number of well-known publishing houses. He has illustrated a number of pet books and nature books as well.

About the Cover Photos

Front cover: These puppies show active interest in their surroundings.

Back cover: This puppy is showing its awareness of its environment.

English translation © Copyright 1998 by Barron's Educational Series, Inc.

© 1997 by Gräfe und Unzer Verlag GmbH, München

Published originally under the title *Unser Welpe*

All rights reserved.

All inquiries should be addressed to:
Barron's Educational Series, Inc.
250 Wireless Boulevard
Hauppauge, New York 11788
http://www.barronseduc.com

Library of Congress Catalog Card No. 98-13990

International Standard Book Number 0-7641-0563-9

Library of Congress Cataloging-in-Publication Data
Schlegl-Kofler, Katharina.
    [Unser welpe.   English]
    Your puppy : expert advice on selecting a puppy, helping it adapt, caring for it, and feeding it / Katharina Schlegl-Kofler ; with color photographs by Christine Steimer ; drawings by György Jankovics.
       p.   cm.
    Includes bibliographical references and index.
    ISBN 0-7641-0563-9
    1. Puppies. I. Title.
SF427.S34413   1998
636.7'07—dc21
                                     98-13990
                                     CIP

Printed in Hong Kong

9 8 7 6 5 4 3 2 1

Encounters with adult dogs are important for a puppy's development. Not all full-grown dogs, however, will put up with having their tails pulled as good naturedly as this one. In a moment, the big dog will show the little one just who has to respect whom here.